THE BLUEPRINTS OF GOD
Science and Math Encoded in the Bible

Roberta Ruth Hill

ACKNOWLEDGEMENTS

Thanks to God, Jesus Christ, the Holy Spirit & the Angels.

Thanks to Kenny and Stella Forinash for editing this book.

CHAPTERS

THE BLUEPRINTS OF GOD

Don't get set into one form, adapt it and build your own, and let it grow, be like water. Empty your mind, be formless, shapeless — like water. Now you put water in a cup, it becomes the cup; You put water into a bottle it becomes the bottle; You put it in a teapot, it becomes the teapot. Now water can flow or it can crash. Be water, my friend. **–Bruce Lee**

The Bible is loaded with many blueprints and intricate designs that form very detailed schematics in the universal languages of science and math. It is interesting and somewhat perplexing that many people are not taught to read the Bible from this higher level of understanding. It is the scientific and mathematical language that explains God's universe in a way that is clearly irrefutable proof as to the truth of God's Word. To read the Bible from just strictly a literal point of view is likened to a child that is just learning to read books for the first time, although the child is learning the basics of reading the words they still do not understand the more complex examples of allegory, metaphors and the more complex symbolic undertones within the stories. Reading the Bible from the symbolic level helps us to gain a better understanding of the stories in the Bible, and perhaps the most valuable symbolic way of reading the Bible is to look at everything from a scientific and mathematical perspective. Science and math can not lie and are the most direct proof to show Divine design.

The first time that I read the entire Bible of the Old Testament and the New Testament, I knew that reading it strictly from a literal standpoint was just not enough to understanding God's Word. As a child, I had read the stories of the Bible from just this viewpoint, and I was able to learn a great deal in that way, but as an adult I couldn't help but see the gaps and holes in reading it from just strictly a literal point of view. Just reading at that level alone causes a lot of contradictions in God's Word, and God can't contradict his words. When you read the Bible, it is quite impossible to read it without thinking and pondering on the diverse meanings. The Bible is the kind of book that grows with the person, and it is not stationary like an object, its words are more like a fluid or water. It changes directions and flows into diverse places.....it ebbs and wanes like the tides of our seas. Like water, God's word is sometimes a fluid which flows freely, and sometimes it is frozen into a block of ice that is no longer mutable. At other times God's Word is similar to steam that rises beyond the physical plane to become invisible within the air. Water is the life force of all life forms and God's Word is the energy force behind all life.

I have learned to look at the higher meanings of the words in the Bible by dissecting the words, looking for anagrams, recognizing the metaphors and homophones and researching about the words themselves. At times the Bible beckons us to look deeper than the actual words that are used and to look at those words from a multi perspective viewpoint. The problem is that we physical humans sometimes turn God's Word into ice when it needs to be a free flowing fluid that can fit into any situation or environment. God's Word is sometimes like ice and immutable, but at other times it very much needs to flow boundlessly like the waters of some gigantic sea, and the words need to mix harmoniously together with other verses to create a more complex view of our world. It is this complexity of God's Word that creates different religions and diverse Christian churches to argue over the meanings of specific stories or verses in the Bible. I have come to see that the Bible's words are more meaningful and fulfilling when we come to accept all unique viewpoints and perspectives to contain some truth to them. In this way, every religion or Christian church does have the truth from their own special perspective. It's just up to us to be able to move like water in our thoughts and just let our ideas and perspectives flow freely into all forms of thought. Instead of putting up dams to try to contain the water, we need to just let it flow naturally and see where we end up. The conflicts of different religions and the diverse denominations of Christian churches have set up dams within the flow of God's Word, because they could not allow other perspectives to enter into their thought processes, and in this way they have turned God's Word into ice that can not flow and has to stay contained within one unchangeable point of view. A square block of ice can not fit into a bowl because it is not round…..it simply will not fit unless we heat that ice block into liquid water that is free flowing. This is the problem with us three dimensional humans, we tend to get stuck on only one thought process, and therefore we blind ourselves to all other realities or perspectives to God's Word. This is where conflict has arisen within the fabric of all religions, which causes tears and rips to divide us from one another. Humans argue over their perspective of God and over their viewpoint on his words. We put up our dams in the rivers of all thoughts, and we try to control the fluid of thought as if it can be controlled into only one thought pattern, then we will tell others that this one perspective is correct. Meanwhile, we have impeded God's Word from flowing downstream the way it should, and it gets controlled and used for whatever purpose we desire.

We often make dams in this physical world to prevent flooding, to store water and to make energy. These are all useful things, and one perspective can argue in that favor, but the other side would argue that now some people don't have enough water downstream, and they have stopped the fish from spawning downstream which effects the fisherman. Dams can be useful in one way and destructive in another. If we picture God's word to be like water or a fluid flowing freely, then we can also picture the different religions or denominations of Christian churches to be the dams. They're useful in some ways and help many people, but in other ways they cause destructive viewpoints to God's Word that damages the multi perspective viewpoints.

We can also think of God's Word as being like a feast in an all you can eat buffet. We get to pick and choose which foods we want to eat based on our own taste preferences. Perhaps my favorite foods are Italian over American foods, or maybe I like Mexican food better than Chinese food. I get to decide what I want to eat, because it is my body. Most of us usually go for a combination of different cultures of foods, so we would sample from all nations delicacies rather than stick with only one kind.

Well, most people are like that with religions, as well. None of us completely believe alike and even those people that are in the same religions have different beliefs from one another. We all tend to pick the ideas and perspectives that we like the best and that we can relate to the most. Here is the problem, we make those decisions based upon the cultures that we were raised in, the environment that we grew up within, the nation that indoctrinated us, the religion or religions that we were exposed to and based on the fads and popular culture of our time. Our perspectives are based on those influences in our life. These are the dams to our thought processes, and they will shape and control our thoughts like a dam controls the water.

Sometimes though as we grow older we tend to take in new perspectives and allow new ideas to reshape our thoughts and form new viewpoints. During these times, we may remove dams or build new ones, but at least we are changing the flow of the water and allowing new shapes to form in our consciousness. We build and destroy at the same time as we try to shape just what we believe and what we don't believe.

For me, I have discovered over the years that when I started taking in new spiritual perspectives that I would learn more and gather more pieces to the puzzles and mysteries of this life as we know it. I was not raised within the confines of a religion, because my parents were raised as Jehovah's Witnesses, and they left that religion when I was a baby. They raised my sister and me with a Christian perspective, but yet they let us explore whatever we wanted to learn. I never remember them ever limiting my exposure to other cultures or religions, and I used to read all kinds of metaphysical books that looked into all of the mysteries on this Earth. They let me read whatever I wanted to read, no matter how odd the subjects. This was a great freedom to me, but at the time I did not realize how precious a gift that was for me to receive from them. I was also blessed to have a mother that understood about my spiritual experiences. and that they were real. Many parents impede their children's spiritual experiences when they tell them that they only imagined seeing an Angel or by telling them that what sometimes happens in their dreams are not real. These parents do not realize when they downplay these spiritual experiences that they are putting up dams to prevent the child from connecting with the spiritual world. If they are told it is not real, then they will be blinded from that reality.

This is the interesting thing about reality. Reality is an illusion, because we are told from the time we were very little about what is real and what is not. Our newspapers, TV's, radios and computers are always telling us what the news is from their own point of view, and we sometimes accept their point of view and make it into our own. But reality is shaped and sculpted by public opinion and the media, and sometimes just because one perspective is more popular than another perspective does not mean that one viewpoint is more real than the other. Both perspectives are just as real, but we have to be able to take the time to explore them both.

The Bible was written from a multi perspective view. We must think of the Bible as being like a TV with a satellite or cable box or like a computer with an internet connection. There are many different channels or websites to consider on the TV or computer. We usually decide which program or website to view based upon the mood that we are in at the time or based on what is available to us. We may read one story in the Bible from a literal individual perspective one day and from a symbolic perspective another day depending on our mood. Reading the Bible and looking at the many different perspectives of a story is like changing the channel on the TV to see what else is on. Maybe one day you're in a sci-fi mood or another day you're in a drama mood, and at other times you just need a comedy to cheer you up. Well, all of those perspectives or genres are on your TV, so all you have to do is tune into the right station to view what you want to see. We tune out or change the channel when we don't want to see a program that we're not in the mood for or that we do not understand.

It is the same way with reading, because we only choose books that are about subjects that we are interested in at the time. Well, the Bible has many different subjects scattered all throughout the books, but many do not even recognize all of the subjects that are in there. This is a problem, because recognizing the different subjects can only be recognized based on your own narrow experiences or perspectives. So, the more you widen your perspectives, and the more experiences you've gained as you get older will lead you to start to notice more layers in the Bible that you never noticed before. All of those layers were always there, but you just needed to be able to recognize them all.

On the TV or the computer, we tune into specific subjects or stories based on certain genres or categories. We have a range of every subject we can think of these days, and the TV has channels on cooking, sci-fi, biography, history, science, comedy, drama, shopping, home improvement, spiritual topics etc., but we have to tune into the program we want when we want to view that particular show or movie. We have to know what and where the channels are to view them. For instance, you might be interested in science, but with the 150 channels you don't know where to find it or perhaps your satellite or cable provider doesn't provide that channel or it isn't in your package. These are the obstacles to finding the perspective that you are in the mood to view.

In the Bible, we have to know where to find certain subjects that we are interested in, and we also have to know quite a few things about that subject to be able to recognize that layer of information. If we don't thoroughly know that subject, then we may miss some clues in the Bible, so knowing the subject matter is a big part to knowing where to find a topic in the Bible. The more you know about the subject, than the more verses you will find relevant to that topic. This is how the Bible grows with you, so that it is not static like a first grade reader. As you learned to read as a child, there were specific books tailored for your reading level, but once you went beyond that reading level you became bored with that lower reading level. For instance, it would be hard as an adult to go back to reading, "Dick and Jane played in the yard". We simply can't go backwards like that after we graduate to a higher level of reading, unless we are reading to a child. Once you graduate to higher levels of reading the Bible, it opens up new layers to explore. It would be like going from a TV with an antenna for broadcast channels to going to a TV with satellite or cable. As you get older and learn more, you will start to find new layers to the books of the Bible, and once you do it's impossible to ignore those new layers. You will see them everywhere!

Reading the Bible from higher perspectives or matrixes of thought is like being able to pick up your remote control and scroll through the many channels at the flick of a button or being able to get on Google and search up thousands of subjects with a click of the mouse. You can literally switch your perspectives on a single story and find many different layers of information to explore based on just shifting your perspective to another view. On TV we can change channels, but in the Bible we can change our perspectives to get a whole new story.

If you have ever looked at a Necker cube or the two faces verses two vases illusion graphics, then you understand what I mean by being able to shift to another perspective to see the graphic in a new and stimulating way. In a Necker cube you can see the cube facing one way and then shift your perception to see the cube facing another way. It is the same with the two faces diagram, sometimes you only see the two faces, and at other times you only see the two vases, but it is very hard to see both the two faces and the two vases at one time. You have to keep shifting back and forth between the two views. Having multiple perspectives is simply like changing or shifting your consciousness to see what else you can find. If you only view one perspective or viewpoint, you become static or stuck and it would be like being stuck on just a narrow range of channels on your TV as opposed to having a large amount of channels to explore.

To be able to explore the scientific and mathematical levels of the Bible you have to become educated about many different subjects. The Bible is constantly giving us clues as to what to look for, but we have to have the curiosity of a child to find them. There is a quote that says "A child can ask questions that a wise man can't answer", and we all know that a child is just naturally curious about everything. Their minds are like a sponge just waiting to absorb every kind of knowledge you have to offer them. It helps when reading the Bible from a scientific perspective to ask many childlike questions. For example, in Genesis 1:2 we are told that the Spirit of God moved upon the face of the water. A child would probably ask "What is the Spirit of God?" or "How can water have a face?" and maybe "What does the face of water look like?" These are questions that can be answered and should be taught to our kids and to adults, as well. These questions can only be answered in a scientific matter to get to the most complete truth. If you tried to answer these questions from a philosophical or even from a literal viewpoint, than you might be able to reveal some perspectives worth finding; however, with science you will find that every answer is the same. If everyone looked at the face of water from a literal viewpoint, we would all say the water looks like us, because it mirrors our image. Now from a scientific perspective, we would actually take a closer look at water to see what the face of water looks like. The answer to that puzzle comes from Job 38:30 where it says the face of the deep is frozen, so we would study a frozen water crystal to see the face of water.

There are perspectives in the Bible that go well beyond our three dimensional universe, but because our viewpoint is so ingrained in three dimensional physics and geometry we fail to recognize the examples of other hyperdimensional realities. Unfortunately, this is just a matter of reading in the Bible from our own three dimensional perspective. We assume that God's Word is only for our third dimensional reality, and in doing so we fail to recognize the other realities that are being presented before our eyes. Recognizing that other dimensions of reality exist beyond our own reality of perception is the key to understanding how to peer into other realities beyond this one that are being presented in the Bible.

A cartoon flip book demonstrates this principal quite simply. If you flip each page at a constant rate, then you get to see a neat animated clip or movie; however, if you flip the pages too fast, you will only see a blur or invisible pages. We could think of the motion created by flipping the pages, as being the vibratory rate of a human being and the dimensions by which the being encounters. If we don't flip the first page, then we are focusing on a two dimensional object and therefore we are stuck in a two dimensional reality. Now how do we get unstuck from this reality? Well, we must start flipping the pages quickly, and then we find that we are encountering something that we have not been exposed to before. We start to see the concept of motion, time and the new dimension of height. This isn't just one two dimensional page, but we find that there are other pages behind the first one and so height gets added to our page, and it becomes an actual book. We can experience this for awhile and focus on this steady rate of vibration in flipping the pages at a constant speed. We get to see things like motion and time in this three dimensional book, and all of these concepts are quite real in our universe. Again though, we can start to get stuck in this reality until that is all that we are focusing on, and we can't see any more realities than this one. We can switch back and forth between the second dimension and the third dimension, but we can't quite see into a higher dimension yet. Death would kind of be like coming to the end of the book, and being unable to flip anymore pages. Without flipping the pages, there is no more time or motion, so you might want to go back to the first page and try to flip again even faster to see if there might be something that you missed in this book of life. Now you could start to flip the pages really fast and at a higher vibration of speed, and what you find out is that everything disappears, as if by some magic trick. This would be the fourth dimension and in this one you can't even measure motion or time, so this would be like the end of time. Linear time is only a reality in the third dimension, but as we break away from this dimension and go into the next one, time will not exist. If you can't see the motion of an object, then you can't measure time. Another trick of going from the third dimension to the fourth dimension is that you would effectively leave the darkness behind, because the illusion of the darkness is caused by the blocking of light from a physical object. The fourth dimension would absolutely be a dimension of light. If you could flip the pages very fast in this book, then the actual book would disappear and all you would see would be the light flowing through the book. The actual book of life works in this way, and it is in you and outside of you.

In the fourth dimension you would actually be able to see time as one whole thing, and it would no longer be a linear time in just one direction the way we experience it here in the third dimension. So, in the fourth dimension you could access the past or the future as easily as flipping a book's pages to any chapter that you want to read. This higher perspective in the fourth dimension would therefore turn you into a prophet from the third dimensional perspective, because you would easily be able to predict the future by being able to have access to the entire timeline of the third dimensional universe.

The Bible presents us with other realities or higher dimensions that are well beyond what we can perceive here in this lower dimension. If we learn about physics and math, then we can see that the Bible gives us the scientific clues to other dimensions within some of its verses. The key to seeing the information about other dimensions can only be seen from a scientific perspective level to reveal the true reality of God's Creation. Only this reality has the physical book of life, and the Bible contains the blueprint for that three dimensional book of life, but it also holds the blueprint for dimensions beyond our own 3-D perspective. Ascension is like shifting our consciousness into a new reality, so the harvest is really about shifting our three dimensional perspective into a higher dimensional viewpoint to encounter a new Earth.

There is a documentary called "What the Bleep do we Know!?", and it has an interesting cartoon about other dimensions. The cartoon shows a three dimensional super hero character that travels through a wormhole down into the second dimension to place called Flatland. The super hero starts talking to a circle lady that lives in a rectangle house. The circle lady can't see the man that is talking, because she can't yet recognize the third dimension. She hears him talking, and she becomes afraid, so she questions whether this is a real conversation or whether he is a ghost. The super hero attempts to give her proof that he is real and tries to explain that he is the same as she; however, he is just in a higher dimension than her dimension, and he can see things in a different way than she does. He decides to give her proof by explaining what she has in a closed off room in the house. From his perspective he is above the two dimensional house made of simple lines, and he can easily see everything in her house, because there are no walls or a roof. Once he tells her everything that is in that room, she becomes convinced that he is real and that he can see things in a different way than she can. At some point the super hero decides that she is ready to actually experience three dimensions, and he pulls her circle form upwards into a sphere. She suddenly looks down upon her entire house for the first time and sees everything from the perspective of the 3-D super hero. She gasps with excitement and proclaims that "she never knew". This is how it would be for us if we were able to suddenly shift our consciousness into a higher dimension, because suddenly everything that we ever thought we knew would change completely into something more than we could ever imagine.

We can begin to see more information in the Bible by only choosing to shift our perspective of it from just viewing it as being a book of morals with the history and genealogy of the Israelite people to seeing it as also being a scientific and mathematical encyclopedia as well. It is through this higher level that we can get substantial proof that the Bible is the word of God. The proven laws and rules of science and the precise mathematical principles of the universe can not lie for their rules are written in stone and are unbreakable. These scientific and mathematical roots are how God created the Tree of Life, and they are the underlying energy for the foundation of everything that we experience here. If you add one plus one, then you must always get two. Math is precise and accurate, which means that you can't ever have the rules change; therefore, the mathematical language is filled with pure truth, which is completely unbreakable in this three dimensional universe. Math and science are likened to the frozen water of thought, because the computations or laws always remain the same within this three dimensional paradigm. Perhaps the laws of science or the mathematical processes we use now could change in other dimensions, but in our dimension these two languages are unbending or unwavering in their principles.

There is another level to the Bible that was discovered by Dean Coombs. He has found hidden messages by simply reading the Hebrew letters in circles or spirals. This code was discovered encoded in Daniel 5, when Mr. Coombs discovered that the writing on the wall that Daniel saw had an encoded message on another way to read the verses. He discovered a hidden message that said to "Go Around". He looked at the scriptures and realized that Daniel 5:25 was talking about 3 ancient Babylonian coins called shekels. The verse says, *"And this is the writing that was written, Mene, Mene, Tekel, Upharsin"*. He started to read the Hebrew as if looking at them around the coins. This had him reading the scriptures in circles to find additional verses that are not discernable from reading the Hebrew from the right to the left. He started to realize that also there were pictograms or pictures associated with reading from this perspective. It's amazing that reading the scriptures in this way gives actual pictures to complement the words of the Bible. This adds an interesting visual component or level to the stories in the Bible, and it shows a more creative side to the Words of God than we could have ever imagined. It shows that all of God's Word is more complex than the actual surface words that were used. They say "a picture is worth a thousand words", so God has used them to add to the authenticity that these are indeed his Words. The complexity of God's Word being told at many different levels of perception would be, in my opinion, impossible for mankind to write.

Another creative level to the Bible is even more astounding than the pictures. Mr. Coombs found that some of these pictures were repeated in other areas, but with a slight change done to the mirror pictures. There is one picture that shows a hand pointing to the right and the other mirror image shows the hand moved more towards the right. When he put these two pictures together, it formed an animated clip of the hand moving to the right. This level of the Bible contains actual animated clips or video. Who could have ever dreamed that the Bible would be so complex and creative at the same time?

The Bible is now starting to look more like an electronic encyclopedia with both pictures and video to accommodate the words. In the book and movie, "Contact" by Carl Sagan, a message is received through a radio telescope from a faraway extraterrestrial civilization. The complexity of the audio message involved encoding prime numbers, audio and video, blueprints, geometry and binary code. The Bible has all of those things and more. The Bible could be thought of as being similar to the volumes of an encyclopedia, but all woven into only one book. God designed the Bible's words to be layered with different kinds of information under many different subjects by using the same space of words to convey many different forms of information. He uses his Words in a multi-perspective way all jumbled into one book in such a complex way that has never been seen before. It would be impossible for mankind to write a story that is layered with math, science, pictures, video, and symbolism, and yet make that story sensible from a literal perspective. I can't even begin to imagine writing at that kind of complexity, yet this is what God does in the Bible.

There is a scene in the movie "Contact", where Hadden gives the solution to find the primer in the pages that was sent to them through the radio telescope. He shows her that the 3 pages line up together only when viewed in three dimensions. If you watch that scene carefully you will see that six pages form a cube, and this is when they could view the primer. Well, the Bible also has a lot of geometry encoded within its words, but many people fail to realize all of the geometry encoded within its stories. It is interesting to know that it describes the same geometrical shapes in many diverse ways, but only for those who have eyes to see it clearly. When Jesus said *"But blessed are your eyes, for they see: and your ears, for they hear"*, he was referring to being able to change your perspective to see the underlying information that is encoded into the story. Many times the words of the

Bible seem to be beckoning us to explore the verse further to unlock all the mysteries that it contains.

The geometry of circles, cubes, triangles, hexagons, tetrahedrons, the Star of David, hypercube and star tetrahedrons are all encoded into various verses and chapters of the Bible. Most people fail to see the clues, but I have found it all over the place in the Bible's stories. At this level, it is wise to have an understanding of sacred geometry and the science of Cymatics. In the beginning was the Word of God, so it is interesting that sound and geometry are infinitely connected with our three dimensional universe, and the Bible very clearly shows us this connection over and over again.

The next level of the Bible is an interactive one. Parables and riddles are designed in such a way to get you to think. This level allows people to participate in a purely interactive way, and this turns the Bible stories into an exercise for the mind. Tell a story in a room full of people, and many different people will share their different perspectives of the story. Most people tend to think that the parable can only mean one thing, but the Bible was not designed in that way. The Bible beckons us to unlock its secrets and keys by challenging people to look at the information from many different viewpoints. As I said earlier in this chapter, many religions try to only allow one perspective by ignoring the other viewpoints that could be just as valid as their own. This sets up dams along the ever flowing beauty of the stories and it prevents people from grasping the multi-perspective view of the scriptures. This can lead to a very stagnant point of view.

Another level of reading the Bible has become quite popular in the last 20 years or so. In Hebrew and Greek the letters are also numbers, so people are using the number equivalent of the letters to add up the total of words and verses. Some interesting developments have come from using this method to prove the authenticity of the Bible being God's Word. The first verse in the Bible has seven words in Hebrew, and it was discovered by Ivan Panin that there are 50 multiples of seven in the very first verse of the Bible. The seven connections seem to strengthen the creation story, which tells us that the Heavens and Earth were made in seven days. Many Bible scholars have discovered some very interesting things by adding up the numbers of words and verses in the Bible. In some instances, it is the practice of Gematria that has given evidence to verify what a verse is referring to and to add further proof. In Isaiah 19:19, all of the Hebrew letters add up to 5449, which is the exact height of the Great Pyramid in inches. This adds another level to the Bible that gives additional information to confirm and add evidence to God's Word.

It is only when we view the Bible from many different perspectives and view its words from many diverse levels of interpretation that we start to see just how complex God's Word can be. The Bible was designed to grow with us as our consciousness grows, and therefore there is always something new to find within its pages. It is simply not the kind of book that you can just read one time and get all the answers you need. It is a workbook for your life, and within its pages you can find the answers to almost anything that you seek to find. It is only a matter of learning how to shift your perspective to find those answers. Those that truly do learn how to be like water, by allowing your consciousness to flow like a liquid, will be the ones that will discover the fullness that the Bible has to offer. It is important to ask those curious childlike questions to see where they may lead, because children are open to every possibility that enters their mind. It's unfortunate that as adults, we have already been brainwashed and indoctrinated to only believe what we are taught, but children come into this world with an open mind. As Bruce Lee said "You put water into a bottle it becomes the bottle; You put it in a teapot it becomes the teapot", so water is flexible and able to change its form to accommodate any container. If you let your consciousness be like water, then you will be flexible enough to learn the stories from a multi-perspective viewpoint. It is through this viewpoint that you will discover so much more than you would have even thought could be possible. Let your journey begin!

WATER

Genesis 1:2 And the earth was without form, and void; and darkness was upon the face of the deep. And the Spirit of God moved upon the face of the waters.

There are a lot of sacred geometry clues in the Bible and the first clue comes from the second verse in the Bible, which is where it says that the Spirit of God moved on the face of the waters. A child may be inclined to ask "What is the face of the water". Let's explore this question and see what comes up. First of all you could take the child to a pond or lake and have them look upon the water to see what clues they can find. Once the child looks at the water he or she will notice himself or herself staring back, because we all know that water acts like a mirror and reflects everything around its surface. The child in their naivety might infer that the face of water is their face since that is the only face that he or she will be able to see. So, if the face of water is like a mirror, than how do we determine what the true face of water really looks like, since water reflects everything?

In the book of Job, there are several clues to help people find the face of the water. These clues are written from a scientific point of view, and it would require a specific tool of science to discover their true meaning. The Lord talks to Job out of a whirlwind and asks him some very deeply thought provoking questions. Many of these questions can only be answered with science, but many religious institutions will not teach the Bible's scriptures from this perspective. First, let us ponder the question in Job 38:22, which says "*Hast thou entered into the treasures of the snow? or hast thou seen the treasures of the hail?*" In our modern times, we can all reply, "yes, we've seen the treasure of the snow." Everyone has been taught in our modern schools what a snowflake looks like, so we have all seen the symmetrical beauty of a water crystal. But let us remember that in Job's time there were no microscopes to view this hidden treasure. The microscope was first invented in 1590 by Hans and Zacharias Janssen. The second clue that the Lord gives to Job is located in verse 30 of Job 38, as the Lord tells Job the solution in finding the treasure of the snow and hail. He says, "The waters are hid as with a stone, and the face of the deep is frozen." It is only in our modern times that we can clearly understand what this means, as the Lord clearly states that you can only see the face of water when it is frozen. If we look at snow under a microscope, then we will indeed see a very beautiful treasure hidden within the water. Even though the microscope was invented in 1590, it would not be until January 15, 1885 before the image of a snowflake could be photographed for the first time, and that photos could now be widely distributed and put into books so that people could now see the face of the water. Wilson Alwyn Bentley was the first person to take a photograph of a snowflake. He would photograph the snowflake on soft black velvet in such a way that their images could be captured before they melted away.

Snowflake photos by Wilson Bentley circa 1902

Within these crystallized patterns are two images that have become associated with the Jewish, Christian and Muslim religions. All snowflakes and ice crystals are in a 6 sided hexagonal form, and we shall see that the hexagon shape is the most revered geometrical shape in the Bible. This shape is featured all throughout the Bible over and over again in many different ways, but the first example is shown in the water because the Spirit of God moved upon its surface. Human beings are approximately 70% water, so our very lives are not only dependent upon water, but we are made of it too. The face of water contains the Star of David and the Holy of Holies cube if you trace it out.

**Star of David   Holy of Holies
Cube**

16

We can clearly see in the image above that the two main images of the Jewish religion is found within the frozen water crystal, so we now know that there is a reason for this ancient geometrical shape to be included with the 3 main religions that were formed from the Bible.

It is no coincidence that the Holy of Holies in the Tabernacle and the Temple is cube shaped. In the Tabernacle the HOH was 10 cubits by 10 cubits by 10 cubits, and in Solomon's Temple the HOH was 20 cubits by 20 cubits by 20 cubits. In 1 Kings 6:20, the verse says, "And the oracle in the forepart was twenty cubits in length, and twenty cubits in breadth, and twenty cubits in the height thereof." The measurement of the Holy of Holies forms a perfect cube, and it is quite obvious that the measurement of cubit contains the clue that we need to cube it. The cube is often associated with perfection, because every side of a cube is of an equal length, width and height, as well as every angle in a cube is at a right angle of 90 degrees.

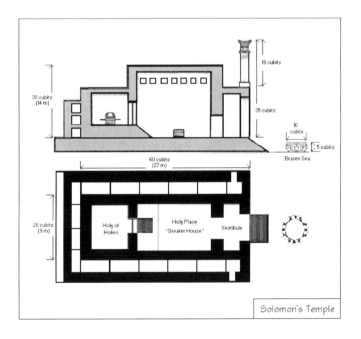

The Holy of Holies cube is another example of the face of water, and water plays an intricate role in most stories of the Bible. The Spirit of God moves upon the face of the water, and water baptism in the ancient biblical days is associated with rebirth or repentance. In Matthew 3:11, John the Baptist says, "I indeed baptize you with water unto repentance: but he that cometh after me is mightier than I, whose shoes I am not worthy to bear: he shall baptize you with the Holy Ghost, and [with] fire." After Jesus Christ, people began to be baptized with the fire of the Holy Ghost, and so we see a reversal in how water baptism required body immersion in water, and fire baptism is the Holy Spirit dipping into the body that is filled with 70% water. If you place fire under the water, than what happens to the water? We all know that boiling water creates steam which is water vapor in a gas form that ascends upward towards the sky or heavens. This is a clue to ascension.

Another clue that is used to show the hexagon shape is the crystal or gemstones in their crystalline form. In Rev. 4:6, it says "And before the throne there was a sea of glass like unto crystal: and in the midst of the throne, and round about the throne, were four beasts full of eyes before and behind". You can clearly see that this verse is comparing the sea or water to being like a crystal. In scientific studies, we learn that crystals form as water evaporates from the internal spaces of the stones, so again we can see a connection between crystals and water. A clear quartz crystal is in the shape of a hexagon, so we can see once again that the Bible is hinting around about the hexagonal nature of water.

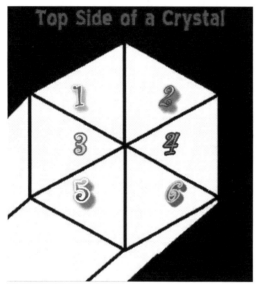 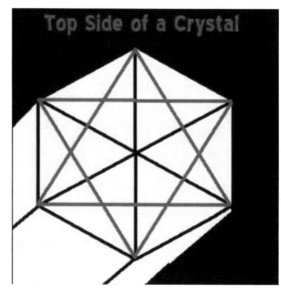

There is one more template that hints around about the hexagon, but this example is a little more complex to find. In Leviticus 20:24, the Lord says to the Israelites *"But I have said unto you, Ye shall inherit their land, and I will give it unto you to possess it, a land that floweth with milk and honey: I am the Lord your God, which have separated you from other people"*. The land of Israel is constantly called the land of milk and honey, so if you research about honey, then you will find the hexagon shape once again. It's interesting to note that all bees make their honey in hexagonal wax compartments that make up a honeycomb. There is another verse that seems to compare the tribe of Judah to the bees. In Judges 14:8 the verse says *"And after a time he returned to take her, and he turned aside to see the carcase of the lion: and, behold, there was a swarm of bees and honey in the carcase of the lion."* The lion is the animal totem of the tribe of

Judah, and Jesus Christ is a descendant of King David from the tribe of Judah.

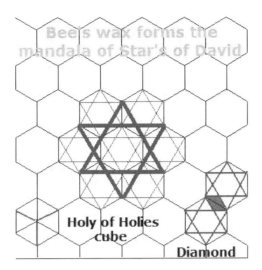

Another example of this pattern of water can be found in the John 21 story, which is about the Apostles fishing with a net and catching 153 fish. This story incorporates the Star of David into the hexagonal pattern of a frozen water crystal. This story shows the beautiful pattern of the equilateral triangles hidden within a hexagon to create the Star of David, and the story does a beautiful job of tying in this hexagon to the water of the sea.

This paragraph offers an interesting side note to the complexity of water. As water mirrors our world in its reflections, it is interesting to know that it also mirrors our emotions, as well. Dr. Masaru Emoto has been photographing ice water crystals for years. He has successfully proven that prayer, words, emotions and music can have either a positive or negative affect on water. He looked at polluted water and saw no crystals at all, but when he offered a prayer for the water and relooked at it under a microscope he found the most beautiful water crystal. This is evidence that water does respond favorably to prayer and positive words. If water can be healed through prayer and positive words, then just imagine how it can heal us, since we all have approximately 70% water in our bodies. Water is amazing!

Reading the Bible from this geometrical and scientific perspective offers us clues to the way our three dimensional universe works. If we look beyond the surface of the water to peer deep inside, we will find a deeper understanding of ourselves, and likewise if we look beyond the surface text of the Bible to unlock new perspectives we will discover the mysteries of the universe are waiting to be found within God's Word.

THE NUMBER 153

Matthew 13:47 Again, the kingdom of heaven is like unto a net, that was cast into the sea, and gathered of every kind:

The first time I read the John 21 fishing story, I took it very literal and thought that it was just another story that authenticated the fact that Jesus Christ was alive after his death. At some point, I actually decided to research the number 153 on the internet and to my surprise I found out that there were many really significant reasons why that number was brought up in this story. Many times the Bible puts obvious hints right in front of our face, and yet we fail to notice them. There is a reason why people do not recognize the math and science that is encoded into the Bible, and that reason is because we are simply not taught to read the Bible at this level of interpretation. Science and religion have always been at odds with one another, but it doesn't have to be this way. Spirituality and science should be able to coexist together, because they compliment each other beautifully. Both science and religions explain the world around us and how it came to be, so there is no use in arguing for which viewpoint is right or wrong, instead we should seek to combine the two together. Science says that the universe began in the big bang and most religions say that God made the universe from nothing. There is no contradiction in these two theories, because the big bang only explains how the universe started in an explosion, and it does not seek to explain who caused that big bang. Religion explains who caused that explosion, whereas science just explains the big bang itself.

Upon researching the number 153, I learned that the fish symbol that was used to represent Jesus Christ in early Christianity has a ratio of 265:153. The body of the fish is in the shape of a vesica piscis, which is made by the intersection of two circles interlinked together. The John 21 story is about catching 153 fish in a net, so it seems appropriate that the fish symbol has a ratio that contains the number 153.

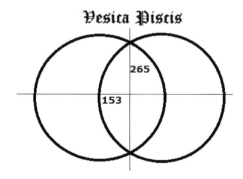

Vesica Piscis

Ratios 265:153 = 1.7320261

The next thing that I researched was about the number 153 being a triangular number. A triangular number is a number that can form a triangle. If you take 153 circles or dots and line them up with each row having one more circle added to each horizontal row and stack them downward, then you will end up with a perfect triangle. This triangle will have 17 dots or circles on each side of the perimeter. It is a perfect equilateral triangle and the vertex should be at a 60 degree angle. The person that made the 153 triangle for Wikipedia did not space out the circles on the base of the left triangle below, so this one is not an equilateral triangle, but the 153 triangle in the image on the right is an equilateral triangle with 60 degree angles on the vertices. The triangle on the left does show that there are 153 circles used to make the 153 triangle.

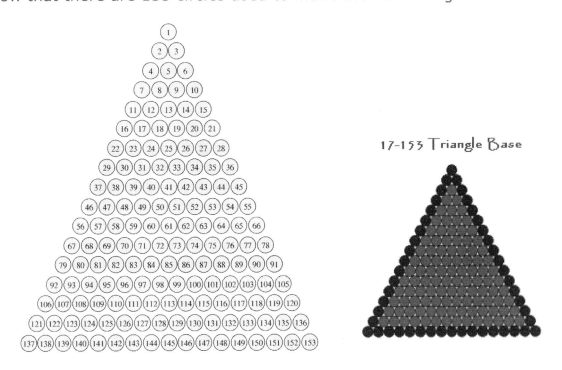

17-153 Triangle Base

As I pointed out earlier, the perimeter of each side contains 17 circles, and this number is closely associated with the number 153 in two ways.

$$17 \times 9 = 153$$

$$1+2+3+4+5+6+7+8+9+10+11+12+13+14+15+16+17=153$$

It's interesting that the 153 triangle has a perimeter on each side that is exactly 17 circles due to the fact that 17 is a divisor into 153 and that the first 17 numbers add up to 153. You can see that the 153 triangle is perfect in every way. This is why the parable fishing story in John 21 is so special. If we look beyond the literal fishing story in John 21, we can see that Jesus

Christ encoded some math lessons for those that have eyes to see and ears to hear. This story is actually showing us a blueprint for the fishing net, and as this chapter continues to progress you will be astonished with all of the information that is encoded in this little story. The unfortunate part of all of this is that most Christian churches are not teaching this parable from a scientific and mathematical level, and therefore most people are ignorant to a much greater story that lies just below the surface of the text and the Sea of Tiberias. Hidden with the number 153 is a powerful message that is just waiting to be discovered by the reader. I like to put myself into each one of the stories of the Bible, because in a sense we are all the characters in the Bible and each story is speaking individually to each and every one of us that are reading its words. In Matthew 4:19, Jesus said to the Apostles *"Follow me, and I will make you fishers of men"*. You can be one of those Apostles that Jesus was speaking to that very day, and you can learn to be a fisher of men as well as learn how to make the net. In this story, Jesus is directly and personally speaking to you. Are you listening?

To continue our lessons to unravel the clues to the information that this geometrical net contains, we must continue to look deeper into the number 153. I also found out that the number 153 is a hexagonal number, as well. This means that if you line up 153 dots into a hexagonal pattern that it will make a perfect hexagon. This is the next big clue to showing us a blueprint of the net.

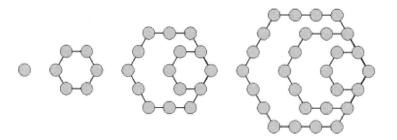

1, 6, 15, 28, 45, 66, 91, 120, 153…

Again, we see the same clue of the hexagon being presented to us. Isn't it interesting that this is the same pattern that can be found in the face of the water? The hexagon contains both the Star of David and the Holy of Holies cube.

You can easily fit a Star of David into a hexagon by forming two triangles by drawing lines to 3 vertices for each one. This stood out to me as being a major clue in the 153 hexagon and the 153 triangle, because the triangle is used to make the Jewish Star of David. In the Star of David a triangle is pointing up and another triangle is pointing down. These 2 triangles are interlocked together to form a 6 pointed star pattern and both triangles are equilateral triangles with a 60 degree angle at each vertex. The triangle pointing up represents the masculine energy and the triangle pointing down represents the feminine energy, so in this way the Star of David is very similar to the Yin/Yang symbol. This star also represents the ancient Hermetic concept of "As above, so below".

Now getting back to triangular numbers, I found out that there is an interesting number pattern that shows how to find all of the triangular numbers. We are not taught this number pattern in school, but we are taught this number pattern in the Bible. If you start adding the numbers together in succession, then you will find that all numbers added together will add up to triangular numbers. It is very interesting to note that all triangles have 3 sides and 3 vertices, and this goes along with the trinity that Christian religions teach. There is the Father, Holy Spirit (some say Mother) and the Son, so the 153 triangle represents all three. There are 2 obvious numbers in the Bible that are triangular numbers, and one of these 2 numbers may surprise you. The 153 triangular number is used to represent Jesus Christ net, and the 666 triangular number represents Satan's net or trap. I was shocked when I first realized that 666 is also a triangular number. If you add the first 36 numbers together, then you will get the number of 666, which is also the number of the beast. You can look at the chart on the next page which shows how it all works out. I also found some other interesting numbers, which I bolded to make them stand out. If you go down 9 rows from the 153 number, then you find the mirror number of 153 which is 351. This playfully teaches us the same concept that we learned in the chapter on water. Jesus net number perfectly mirrors itself in the triangular numbers just as water mirrors us in visual reflections and in our emotions. The other funny thing is the 9 connection to those numbers and the spacing of 9 in between them on the chart (1+5+3=9 or 3+5+1=9). This number chart shows just how special this number is and why it is the number associated with Jesus' fishing net.

I also found out that there is a special relationship between the number 153 and 666. Only one website I found tried to explain this relationship, but at first I was unable to understand what the person was showing on their blog. It took me a few days to completely understand how this relationship works out. I discovered that the numbers of 153 and 666 were mentioned in the

Bible to also display the mathematical anomaly that occurs between these 2 triangular numbers.

All sums are triangular numbers!

```
1+2=3
1+2+3=6
1+2+3+4=10
1+2+3+4+5=15
1+2+3+4+5+6=21
1+2+3+4+5+6+7=28
1+2+3+4+5+6+7+8=36
1+2+3+4+5+6+7+8+9=45
1+2+3+4+5+6+7+8+9+10=55
1+2+3+4+5+6+7+8+9+10+11=66
1+2+3+4+5+6+7+8+9+10+11+12=78
1+2+3+4+5+6+7+8+9+10+11+12+13=91
1+2+3+4+5+6+7+8+9+10+11+12+13+14=105
1+2+3+4+5+6+7+8+9+10+11+12+13+14+15=120
1+2+3+4+5+6+7+8+9+10+11+12+13+14+15+16=136
1+2+3+4+5+6+7+8+9+10+11+12+13+14+15+16+17=153
1+2+3+4+5+6+7+8+9+10+11+12+13+14+15+16+17+18=171
1+2+3+4+5+6+7+8+9+10+11+12+13+14+15+16+17+18+19=190
1+2+3+4+5+6+7+8+9+10+11+12+13+14+15+16+17+18+19+20=210
1+2+3+4+5+6+7+8+9+10+11+12+13+14+15+16+17+18+19+20+21=231
1+2+3+4+5+6+7+8+9+10+11+12+13+14+15+16+17+18+19+20+21+22=253
1+2+3+4+5+6+7+8+9+10+11+12+13+14+15+16+17+18+19+20+21+22+23=276
1+2+3+4+5+6+7+8+9+10+11+12+13+14+15+16+17+18+19+20+21+22+23+24=300
1+2+3+4+5+6+7+8+9+10+11+12+13+14+15+16+17+18+19+20+21+22+23+24+25=325
1+2+3+4+5+6+7+8+9+10+11+12+13+14+15+16+17+18+19+20+21+22+23+24+25+26=351
1+2+3+4+5+6+7+8+9+10+11+12+13+14+15+16+17+18+19+20+21+22+23+24+25+26+27=378
1+2+3+4+5+6+7+8+9+10+11+12+13+14+15+16+17+18+19+20+21+22+23+24+25+26+27+28=406
1+2+3+4+5+6+7+8+9+10+11+12+13+14+15+16+17+18+19+20+21+22+23+24+25+26+27+28+29=435
1+2+3+4+5+6+7+8+9+10+11+12+13+14+15+16+17+18+19+20+21+22+23+24+25+26+27+28+29+30=465
1+2+3+4+5+6+7+8+9+10+11+12+13+14+15+16+17+18+19+20+21+22+23+24+25+26+27+28+29+30+31=496
1+2+3+4+5+6+7+8+9+10+11+12+13+14+15+16+17+18+19+20+21+22+23+24+25+26+27+28+29+30+31+32=528
1+2+3+4+5+6+7+8+9+10+11+12+13+14+15+16+17+18+19+20+21+22+23+24+25+26+27+28+29+30+31+32+33=561
1+2+3+4+5+6+7+8+9+10+11+12+13+14+15+16+17+18+19+20+21+22+23+24+25+26+27+28+29+30+31+32+33+34=595
1+2+3+4+5+6+7+8+9+10+11+12+13+14+15+16+17+18+19+20+21+22+23+24+25+26+27+28+29+30+31+32+33+34+35=630
1+2+3+4+5+6+7+8+9+10+11+12+13+14+15+16+17+18+19+20+21+22+23+24+25+26+27+28+29+30+31+32+33+34+35+36=666
```

The chart above shows the first 36 triangular numbers.

When I first started to explore the connection between the number 153 and 666, I decided to work out the perimeter formula on both the 153 and 666 triangles. To use the perimeter formula, I had to add the sides of the triangle (i.e. A+B+C=). The 153 triangle has 17 circles on each side, so I added them together and got the number 51 (i.e. 17+17+17=51). It's interesting that the number 51 also divides into the number 153, so that was definitely a fascinating correlation. I then decided to work on the perimeter formula on the 666 triangle, and I found out that the sum of its perimeter does not divide into 666, so the 153 triangle is more perfect than the 666 triangle. I added the numbers of the perimeter and got the number 108 (i.e. 36+36+36=108), which interestingly enough also seems to be a significant number in many different religions. There are 108 beads on Hindu and Buddhist malas or rosaries. The most significant fact about this number is that the sun's diameter is 108 times the Earth's diameter. The number 108, and all of its multiples are found throughout the universe, but I am not going to go into detail about the 108 number. Anyway, I divided 666 by 108 and got the number 6.166666666666667, so it does not divide evenly like the 153 triangle and 666 is not a hexagonal number either.

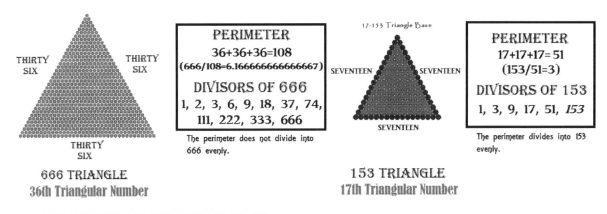

1+2+3+4+5+6+7+8+9+10+11+12+13+14+15+16+17=153
1+2+3+4+5+6+7+8+9+10+11+12+13+14+15+16+17+18+19+20+21+22+23+24+25+26+27+28+29+30+31+32+33+34+35+36=666

A few days later, I realized what the article on a blog was trying to explain about the relationship between the 153 triangle and the 666 triangle. If you count the circles or dots going around both triangles and then add those sums together, you will get the number 153, and only the perimeter sums of these 2 triangles will make the 153 number. This is astounding to me considering the belief among most Christians is that this number represents evil. The 666 number is not evil, but the Bible does say that we can identify the beast with this number. In this case, the number 666 is only being used to find the identity of the beast or antichrist, so it is being used like a name is used to identify a person.

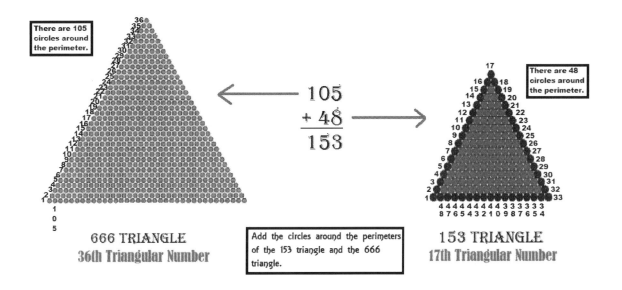

You should be able to see by now that the first 17 verses of John 21 actually contain an encyclopedia amount of information. The key to unlocking that information is to thoroughly research about the number 153, and within that number are vast amounts of geometrical blueprints that were designed by God in the making of this universe. If the Christian religion actually taught the multi-perspective aspects of the fishing story in John 21, then they would be teaching it from a mathematical/geometrical and from a scientific perspective. You could actually use this story to teach kids in school about mathematics, geometry and the physics of energy. The multi-layered information in this one parable alone could probably fill a volume of an encyclopedia, so we can see that this simple fishing story is in all actuality a very complex blueprint to the universe. The Bible is truly an encyclopedia galactica of data that contains the knowledge of the universe.

One thing that I noticed at some point in my research is that the equilateral triangle can be divided evenly into 4 equilateral triangles. The amazing thing about this is that when we do divide a triangle into 4 triangles, then we can now bring this triangle into three dimensions. We can literally raise it up into a tetrahedron shape. A tetrahedron is a three dimensional shape that has four sides made up of equilateral triangles.

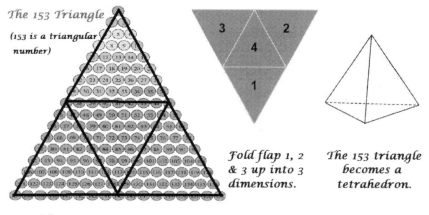

The 153 Triangle
(153 is a triangular number)

Fold flap 1, 2 & 3 up into 3 dimensions.

The 153 triangle becomes a tetrahedron.

Two tetrahedrons form a Merkaba. One is pointing up and one down, and it looks like a two dimensional Star of David from the side.

The #153 Connetion to the Merkaba

As you can see from the graphic above, we can fold flaps 1, 2 and 3 upwards and make a tetrahedron. Now remember 153 is also a hexagonal number and within that hexagon we can make a Star of David which contains 2 triangles. If we carry that template into the third dimension, then the two dimensional Star of David would actually be a star tetrahedron. It's interesting that in spiritual teachings the shape of a Merkaba or light chariot is in the shape of a star tetrahedron. This is actually an energy pattern of light in which each tetrahedron spins in counter rotation to the other. The star tetrahedron is said to be the underlying energy of all objects in our universe. This is where our lesson starts to cross over into the science of physics. Richard C. Hoagland has done research about the star tetrahedron energy pattern of the Earth. He found that the base of each tetrahedron is located at 19.5 degrees on the north and south latitudes.

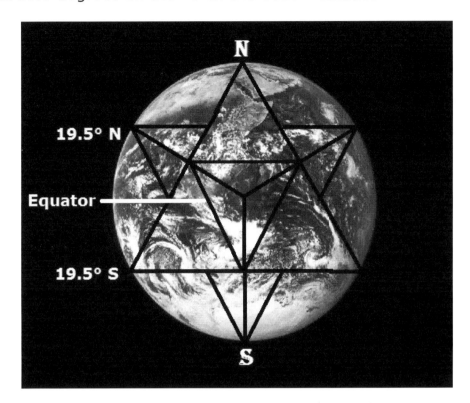

At 19.6 degrees north there is the largest shield volcano on the Earth at Mauna-Kea volcano on the island of Hawaii. A shield volcano is usually built almost entirely of fluid lava flows and it resembles the shape of a warrior's shield. The Mayan ruin of Teotihuacan near Mexico City has a latitude and longitude of 19°41'33"N 98°50'37.68"W, which is very close to this 19.5 degree zone, so perhaps the ancient people were trying to mark out this tetrahedron energy zone.

The underlying energy pattern of the universe is based upon the hexagon shape, and we can see this in the water on a microscopic level, but on a macroscopic level we can see that the energy pattern of all objects in this universe is based upon the star tetrahedron and the hexagonal patterns. The John 21 story is basically describing the energetic patterns of the three dimensional universe. It is astounding to think that this level of the Bible has been hidden from our perspective for thousands of year by religions that sought to control this information and to hide it from the masses. All the while the answers to the universe were hidden in plain sight within the Bible, and those keys could only be understood for those that "have eyes to see and ears to hear", as Jesus would say. It was only a matter of learning to shift our consciousness into new and higher levels or perspectives to unlock the keys to the mysteries of this universe. Reading the Bible from the level of science and math is a new way to read this ancient book.

Before I continue with the number 153, I want to say that I did not discover all of this information on my own. The Holy Spirit has been an intricate part of all of my discoveries on this learning path, and without this instruction I could have never understood the higher meanings contained within the Bible. I am merely a curious student, as everyone else, but at some point a student becomes a teacher, and I love to share what I have learned with anyone that wants to learn also. The Holy Spirit is the best teacher of these mysteries, and I hope that each person reading this book has been able to learn in this way.

Ironically enough, I also learned a lot of information from the net, as well. I'm not talking about the fishing net though; I learned much knowledge from the internet. We are now living in a time that knowledge can easily be shared from around the world and looking up information on the internet is like having all of the world's libraries at your fingertips. It certainly makes me think of the prophetic times of the last days that is talked about in Daniel 12:4, when it says *"But thou, O Daniel, shut up the words, and seal the book, even to the time of the end: many shall run to and fro, and **knowledge shall be increased"**.

Now to continue, the hexagon is associated with a very ancient symbol called the Flower of Life, and this mysterious symbol can be found in the ancient Egyptian, Assyrian, Greek and Jewish cultures. The centerpiece of the Flower of Life is called a Seed of Life, and it consists of 7 circles intersecting one another to form the vesica piscis or fish symbol over and over again until it fits into a hexagon shape. The Seed of Life diagram below depicts the 6 days of creation.

Rotating Octahedron   Spherical Octahedron   Vescia Piscis (1st Day)   Tripod of Life (2nd Day)   (3rd Day)   (4th Day)   (5th Day)   (6th Day)

Mikeoprisko – Wikipedia

The actual Flower of Life builds upon this Seed of Life in the center and extends outward into 3 layers of seeds, and then it is completed by putting a circle around the exterior with 6 points of the hexagon touching the circle's edge.

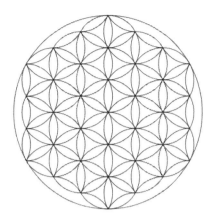

User:Life of Riley – Wikipedia

I looked at this graphic one day and I realized that there were a lot of fish within what actually looks like a hexagon and a circular fishing net. I had the thought to start counting the fish. There were 90 small fish inside the Flower of Life, and I gradually began to shift my perspective to see bigger fish within the net also. Eventually, I saw a graphic on the internet that combined the Flower of Life with the Metatron's cube and I realized that I needed to include the cube and count all of the fish on the outer edge. Once I did that the fish number began to climb to 150 fish. I got to a point where I was stuck on finding the 3 fish that must be there somewhere, and I got frustrated. It was just so close to count 150 fish and to not be able to find the 3 fish anywhere. One day it dawned on me that the 3 fish are made up by the 6 points around the hexagon. I went fishing around to catch me some fish and by the time I had finished, I had finally caught the 153 fish within the net, and I didn't even have to go in the water to catch them.

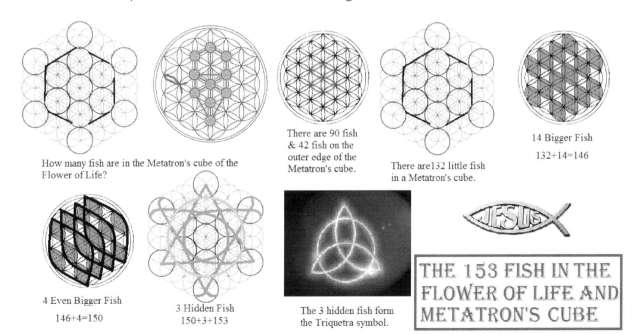

How many fish are in the Metatron's cube of the Flower of Life?

There are 90 fish & 42 fish on the outer edge of the Metatron's cube.

There are 132 little fish in a Metatron's cube.

14 Bigger Fish
132+14=146

4 Even Bigger Fish
146+4=150

3 Hidden Fish
150+3+153

The 3 hidden fish form the Triquetra symbol.

THE 153 FISH IN THE FLOWER OF LIFE AND METATRON'S CUBE

29

I drew the last 3 big fish out, and it made 3 intersecting fish, and I knew that somehow this looked very familiar to me, but I couldn't remember where I had seen this image before. I looked for a long time before I finally found this symbol, and I found out that it was called the Triquetra. I learned that the Triquetra originally referred to the triangle, but now it had become the shape of three vesica piscis. This symbol is also used by Christians to represent the trinity of the Father, Son and the Holy Spirit.

The symbol that I found in the center of the net is very similar to the Triquetra, but the symbol that I drew out seems to look a lot like the Star of David with two triangles. If you look closely at the drawing above, you will see a Star of David in the three fish.

In Isaiah 19:19, it says "*In that day shall there be an altar to the LORD in the midst of the land of Egypt, and a pillar at the border thereof to the LORD*". As I already showed in the first chapter, there is evidence that this verse is referring to the Great Pyramid among the pyramids of Giza in Egypt. I will now show you further evidence that will tie the Great Pyramid into the Bible and specifically into the John 21 fishing story.

List of facts that I have found about the Great Pyramid:

1. The slope of the Great Pyramid is **51** degrees. (51X3=153)
2. The Grand Gallery in the Great Pyramid is **153 feet** long.
3. The main entrance inside the Great Pyramid is at the **17**th level of blocks. (17X9=153 & 1+2+3+4+5+6+7+8+9+10+11+12+13+14+15+16+17=153)
4. The **153rd** course of masonry from the ground, on the outside of the Great Pyramid, is 360 feet above the ground. (360 degrees of a circle)
5. Inside the Great Pyramid, from the King's Chamber floor up to the summit platform there are **153** courses of masonry.

As you can see the number 153 is encoded all throughout the Great Pyramid in many different ways. The Great Pyramid has 4 equilateral triangles on its sides and the base is a perfect square. Each side of the Great Pyramid is clearly representative of the 153 triangle, because the mathematical clues offer evidence that the Great Pyramid or monument to the Lord was encoded with the John 21 story.

I realized at some point that the Tabernacle and Temple also encoded the fishing story of John 21. The first clue can be found in Exodus 27:5 where it says "*And thou shalt put it under the compass of the altar beneath, that the **net** may be even to the midst of the altar*". The net on the Bronze Altar is meant to symbolize the fishing net in John 21. The Bronze Water Laver is also in the courtyard outside of the Tabernacle, and it represents the water or sea where the Apostles are fishing. The Tabernacle also represents a star map, but I will be explaining more about this discovery in another chapter. Anyway, the Table of Shewbread and the 7 candlestick Menorah represents the Pisces constellation with the two fish, so we can see the symbolism of the fish that are being caught in the net. In John 21:8, the verse says "*And the other disciples came in a little ship; (for they were not far from land, but as it were two hundred cubits,) dragging the net with fishes.*" It's interesting to note that the Bronze Altar with the net is located outside of the Tabernacle, and therefore we can see the Tabernacle as representing the ship and the Bronze Altar represents the fishing net. It all fits in beautifully! The Holy of Holies is cube shaped and therefore it represents the Star of David and the star tetrahedron in a three dimensional configuration. This cube shows the 153 triangle and the 153 hexagon from a two dimensional perspective. I got creative and added 2 of the 153 triangles on each end of the Tabernacle to make it look more like a ship with the bow and the stern.

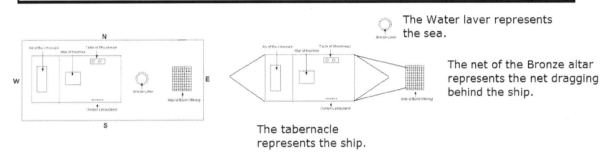

The tabernacle represents the ship.

The net of the Bronze altar represents the net dragging behind the ship.

The Water laver represents the sea.

The Tabernacle had its door facing east towards the rising sun, and that is also prophetic of Jesus Christ ascending or rising in the sky after his death. In John 21:6, Jesus says "**Cast the net on the right side of the ship**, *and ye shall find. They cast therefore, and now they were not able to draw it for the multitude of fishes*". We can see that the net is on the right side of the Tabernacle, because the east side of a compass is always on the right side. So, in this interpretation or perspective of the Tabernacle pattern, we can see that the net was cast out on the right side of the ship. You can clearly see that the John 21 fishing story was embedded into the pattern of the Tabernacle, and it shows the ship dragging the net towards the west. The ship is sailing towards the setting sun or should I say the setting Son. This clearly represents the second coming of Jesus Christ to claim his bride during the harvest or rapture.

I can't help but think about that future day, as I look at this blueprint of John 21. Someday soon the bride will ride on this ship towards the bright light of the setting sun, and she will be moving towards her groom whom is the Son of God. She will be standing on the wedding altar (Incense Altar) towards the middle of this ship as she waits to cross the horizon over to the other side. While standing on the altar, she will alter herself in preparation for the marriage of the Lamb. Both the bride and the groom will go off together into the sunset on a special honeymoon cruise upon the vast cosmic sea, and their destination will be to a faraway place way beyond this dimension. This will be the fairy tale wedding that the bride and groom have always dreamt about together as they go into that netherworld beyond this one to live happily ever after.

Now that we have covered that the equilateral 153 triangle and the 153 hexagon are woven all into God's pattern of this three dimensional universe, I will show you that God put his mark on the 6th planet in our Solar System. It is certainly no coincidence that NASA has photographed a big hexagon on the north pole of Saturn. God made the universe in 6 days, and He rested on the 7th day, so it is quite interesting that God marked the 6th planet with the 6 sided hexagon symbol that represents the Holy of Holies cube and the Star of David simultaneously. I also find it quite interesting that the Jewish Sabbath is on Saturday, because Saturday is named after Saturn.

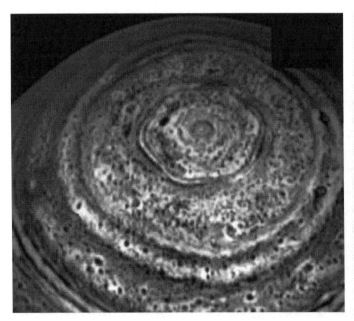 

Surprisingly, the 153 number is also associated with chemistry too. I discovered that in the alchemical process of making the Philosopher's Stone there is a step that is called "The Net", which is a copper-antimony alloy, named for its crystalline "net" like surface. The main element used in this step is Antimony, which has an atomic number of 51. It seems somewhat clever that the alchemist called this step "The Net" considering the fact that they used this name because 153 is divisible by 51 and the John 21 story is all about fishing with a net and catching 153 fish. It became even more interesting when I started to look for all of the metals that were used in the building of the Tabernacle and the Temple in the periodic table and discovered that the four elements could form a triangle that points directly to the 51st element of Antimony. Bronze was an alloy made up of copper and tin in the biblical times, because zinc was not known at those times.

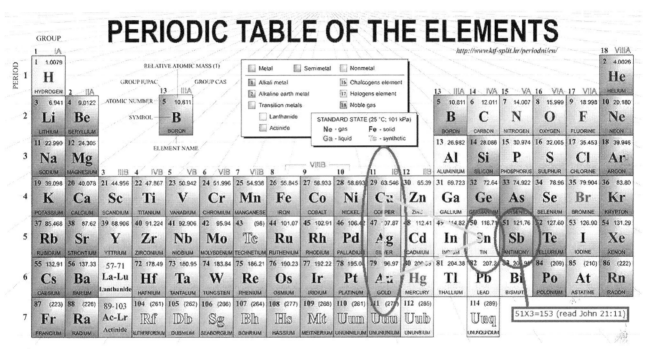

Exodus 25

3 And this is the offering which ye shall take of them; gold, and silver, and brass, (Bronze is an alloy made with copper and tin.)

4 And blue, and purple, and scarlet, and fine linen, and goats' hair,

5 And rams' skins dyed red, and badgers' skins, and shittim wood,

6 Oil for the light, spices for anointing oil, and for sweet incense,

7 Onyx stones, and stones to be set in the ephod, and in the breastplate.

8 And let them make me a sanctuary; that I may dwell among them.

9 According to all that I shew thee, after the pattern of the tabernacle, and the pattern of all the instruments thereof, even so shall ye make it.

This is the 2nd encoded story of the 153 fish in the net that is included in the Tabernacle pattern. The Philosopher's Stone is the white powder gold that was used in the shewbread that the high priest ate in the Tabernacle. It was used to tune the high priest's body for worship in the Tabernacle or the Temple. In the 1970's a farmer named David Hudson rediscovered white powder gold in Arizona. He applied for a patent of his discovery, but to comply with the patent requirement he had to do more research test to provide information of the weight and other measurements. When they heated the substance, they found that the mass of the powder was reduced, and they didn't know why some of the mass had disappeared. Hal Puthoff is the director of the Institute for Advanced studies, and he had determined that when matter reacts in two dimensions it should theoretically lose four-ninths of its gravitational weight, which was the amount of mass that was lost in the heating experiment of white powder gold. The result of their experiments have shown that white powder gold is really exotic matter which is capable of bending space/time and keeping a wormhole open for travel. A wormhole is mostly depicted in physicist models as being like a net, so isn't it interesting that "The Net" process of making the Philosopher's Stone actually leads to making a net of another kind.

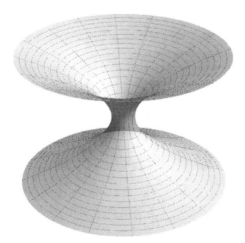

AllenMcC. – Wikipedia

Another topic worth discussing at this point is the subject of near death experiences or NDE's. There have been many people that have died only to be revived back to life with the modern medical technology that we have of our time. There are quite a few people that have described their souls leaving their bodies after they died, and then they feel attracted towards or are pulled into a whirling mass of darkness that seems oddly similar to a black hole. Once they have entered the hole, they begin to travel very quickly down a tunnel towards a light at the end of the tunnel. This tunnel would be considered a traversable wormhole from a physics perspective. I will be discussing more about wormholes that are mentioned in the Bible in another chapter, but for now I wanted to bring out the net connection to wormholes and white powder gold.

I briefly described in the first chapter about the picture Bible code discoveries that were found in the Bible by Dean Coombs. It is interesting to me that one of the pictures found shows the fishing boat and the net of John 21, and it also cleverly hints at a wormhole connection to the net due to two pictures that are overlapping together. The one picture shows a boat with the net thrown into the sea, and the other one shows a prophetess with sun glasses on. The boat overlaps with the throat of the prophetess, and it's interesting that the physicist call the opening to a wormhole a mouth and the tunnel they call a throat.

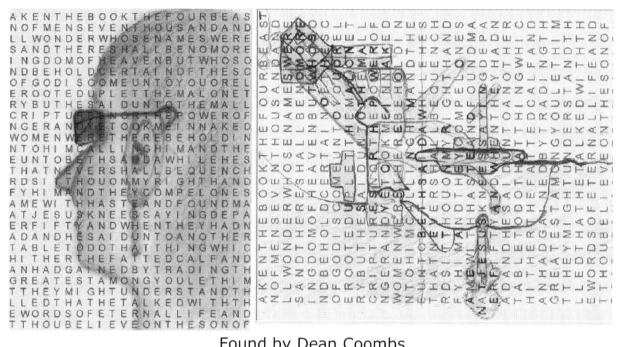

Found by Dean Coombs

As you can see in the overlapping pictures of the prophetess and the boat with the net, the boat has been positioned just inside the mouth and it is getting ready to go down through the throat. There is an analogy being made between the wormholes throat and mouth and the prophetess mouth and throat.

There is a pyramid structure in the background, and it is being mirrored in the water. The base of the pyramid is 17 letters and the height of the pyramid contains 9 letters (17X9=153), so this is perhaps a clue to the Great Pyramid in Egypt. I decided to measure the angle of the pyramid and it was around the 50 degree mark, so perhaps it is meant to be 51 degrees. This is Dean Coombs drawing of the picture of the pyramid, so I would think the shading of the letters forming a pyramid should be at a 51 degree angle to further show the Great Pyramid connection (51X3=153). The boat or ship says "I AM YESHUA", which is Jesus name in Hebrew. A net has been thrown in between the boat that is 9 letters long and the base of the pyramid which is 17 letters long; therefore we can multiply the 9 and 17 to get the amount of fish that is in the net. The net says NETENA, which is "NET" reading it forward from left to right and it says "A NET" reading it in reverse from right to left.

This next interpretation of the John 21 story is quite controversial, but I decided to include it in this book anyway. There is a theory that Jesus married Mary Magdalene and that they had some children together. Many Christians scoff at the idea of Jesus marrying and having children; however God told Abraham in Genesis 35:11 "**be fruitful and multiply**; *a nation and a company of nations shall be of thee, and kings shall come out of thy loins*". It is not a sin to marry and have children, and Jesus being a rabbi would have been expected to marry to fulfill God's commandment to Abraham to be fruitful. There are a lot of books out there that show evidence for Jesus and Mary Magdalene being married, so I will not cover this topic any further. I will leave it up to the reader to decide for him or her self. If you do not believe that Jesus married and had children, then I recommend that you skip reading the rest of this chapter as this information would not interest you.

When I was researching about the various origin theories to the mysterious and rare RH negative blood type, I found an article about the Grail theory. I started researching about the various stories about Mary Magdalene coming to France with a child after Jesus crucifixion, and I found out that she lived not very far from the Basque people of Spain and France. The Basque people are said to have the most of the RH negative blood type in the world, so I found it rather peculiar when I found out the Basque genetic marker had been given the name M153. Immediately, I thought this must be a clue to Jesus' descendants, and I set out to see if there was any more evidence to support my theory. I found out that the Merovingian kings said that they were descendants of Jesus and Mary Magdalene, and you can see that reflected in their name which hints around about the Mary vine. I read the book "The Holy Blood and the Holy Grail" and saw many names that were connected with the Grail legends. My mother was doing family tree research online, and she ran into a branch of Plantagenet kings and queens, and when she showed me that name, I remembered that this name was linked to the Grail bloodline. I decided to help her on this branch to see where it would lead, and it led right straight to the Merovingian kings. At some point, I realized the inside joke on the Plantagenet name, and I realized that perhaps there is another interpretation of the John 21 story. Their name was an anagram for plant-age-net. Was there some kind of net being planted? I wondered. In Matthew 26:28 it says, "*For this is my blood of the new testament, which is shed for many for the remission of sins*". One interpretation of shedding your blood could have to do with shedding your blood onto your children or by passing on the blood in a bloodline. The word San grail was thought to mean "Holy Grail", but if it is broken down into two words Sang raal, then it means "blood royal". The only way to carry royal blood is not in a cup, but in the womb, so this leads to more evidence that Jesus was shedding his royal blood onto his descendants. Perhaps Jesus Christ blood of the New Testament had a genetic change that was done for the purpose of creating a worldwide net for the harvest that is spoken of in the book of Revelation. Maybe the plan was to **plant** the seed and then wait for it to grow in number or **age** over time to make a global **net**. This plan seems to be reflected in the Grail name of Plantagenet. I have wondered if perhaps the Grail bloodline is here to increase the vibratory rate of the planet Earth. There must be a reason for Jesus to shed his blood of the New Testament onto the Grail bloodline.

I recently found the next clue in the John 21 story when I realized that the sea of Tiberias had a very important place to the grail story embedded within the name of the sea that the Apostles fished. The Iberian Peninsula is commonly called Iberia, and it consists of the countries of Spain, Portugal, Andorra and the southern part of France. One day I was looking at the first verse in John 21 that says *"After these things Jesus shewed himself again to the disciples at the sea of Tiberias; and on this wise shewed he himself"*, and I noticed that Iberia was in the word **Tiberia**s. It could just be a coincidence, but I am inclined to think it is not. Perhaps a genetic net was deployed in Iberia to help spread the blood of the New Testament.

Iberia

Well, I've taken you on a mathematical and scientific journey to learn about the net of the harvest. Hidden within the John 21 fishing story is a vast amount of blueprints and information embedded within just 17 verses. It is incredible to think that so much information could be encoded with that one simple story, and how it links to other stories within the Bible and even to the Great Pyramid in Egypt and perhaps to Iberia in Europe. As I have shown you this story is not meant to be taken solely as a literal story, because the meat of the story has to do with the number of fish that is caught.

The literal perspective of the story is likened to a baby that drinks milk for its food, but at some point a baby starts to grow up and needs to eat meat for their meal. Jesus asked in John 21:5, *"Children, have ye any meat?"* This is a clue that there is much more to this story than what appears at the surface. I took you below the surface of the text to fish in this sea of words and showed you the true structure of the net. I showed you the meat in the story and left the milk to the babes.

Hebrews 5:12-13 New English Translation (NET)

[12] For though you should in fact be teachers by this time, you need someone to teach you the beginning elements of God's utterances. You have gone back to needing milk, not solid food.
[13] For everyone who lives on milk is inexperienced in the message of righteousness, because he is an infant.

Jesus asked Peter three times to feed his lambs and his sheep from verse 15 through 17 of John 21. What do you feed the baby lambs, and what do you feed the full grown sheep? I am feeding the sheep their meat to eat. Okay, hidden in verses 14 through 17 is another number clue to the number 153. The last part of the John 21 fishing story keeps hinting around about the number three, when it says this was the third time Jesus showed himself to his disciples, and Jesus tells Peter three times to feed the lambs and sheep. He starts at verse 15 with telling him to feed my lambs and number 51 is the mirror image of 15, so this is another clue to divide 3 into 153 to get 51. On the third time he tells Peter to feed his sheep at verse 17, and if we multiply 17 times 3, then we get 51. Of course, there is also the other connection of 17 to the number 153. These last four verses are merely just showing you the divisors of the number 153. Its simple math problems!

There is another deeper meaning to Jesus asking the Apostles if they have any meat in verse 5. In John 4:33, the disciples asked Jesus if he had eaten, and he replied in John 4:34 "*My meat is to do the will of him that sent me, and to finish his work.*" When he asked the Apostles if they had meat, he was not referring to them fishing for fish so that they could eat. He was telling them two things, and what he was telling them he is also telling us. He is saying to take a look at the deeper meanings or meat of the story and to do the will of the Father by helping to finish God's work. The Apostles are fishers of men, so at this point in time they were not doing man's work of catching fish for meat; instead they were doing God's work and catching men for God.

Hidden within the fabric of this simple fishing story is mathematics, geometry, genetics and physics. It almost seems impossible to put so much information in such a small amount of space and yet can anyone deny that all of this information is there? I've showed you the proof of how everything fits so neatly within the many layers of this story.

We went fishing together, and we caught some meat, so now we need to find the solution on how this information will help us to do God's work. The next chapter will talk about the mysterious Solfeggio tones that were found in the seventh chapter of the book of Numbers. You will get to find out if we will have to sing for our supper, so to speak, to get our meat. I know that sounds cryptic, but follow me on this fishing boat and let us fish around the Bible for the answers.

THE SOLFEGGIO TONES (SONG OF DEGREES)

Revelation 14:3 And they sung as it were a new song before the throne, and before the four beasts, and the elders: and no man could learn that song but the hundred and forty and four thousand, which were redeemed from the earth.

The healing codes or Solfeggio tones were given to Dr. Joseph S. Puleo by Jesus Christ in 1999, the location of the codes can be found in Numbers Chapter 7 in verses 12 through 83. Let me explain. These are more than other hidden Bible codes that people have found; they are not to be used for prophecy or to explain current events. These hidden codes have been revealed at a time in which the Earth and people are going through very stressful changes. These codes reveal six electromagnetic frequencies that have the power to change our lives and heal.

Starting at verse 12 you start using Pythagorean math of reducing the verse numbers to single digits by adding the digits together to reduce it to a single integer. For example, 1+2=3, so the first verse would be a 3. You continue to do this all the way to verse 83, and write out the single digit by every verse. Now go down every 6 verse starting with verse 12 and go to verse 18, then repeat the process by going down to the 6 verse from verse 18. This will give you the first tone in the series.

3 *¹² And he that offered his offering the **first day** was Nahshon the son of Amminadab, of the tribe of Judah:*

4 *¹³ And his offering was one silver charger, the weight thereof was an hundred and thirty shekels, one silver bowl of seventy shekels, after the shekel of the sanctuary; both of them were full of fine flour mingled with oil for a meat offering:*

5 *¹⁴ One spoon of ten shekels of gold, full of incense:*

6 *¹⁵ One young bullock, one ram, one lamb of the first year, for a burnt offering:*

7 *¹⁶ One kid of the goats for a sin offering:*

8 *¹⁷ And for a sacrifice of peace offerings, two oxen, five rams, five he goats, five lambs of the first year: this was the offering of Nahshon the son of Amminadab.*

9 *¹⁸ On the **second day** Nethaneel the son of Zuar, prince of Issachar, did offer:*

1 *¹⁹ He offered for his offering one silver charger, the weight whereof was an hundred and thirty shekels, one silver bowl of seventy shekels, after the shekel of the sanctuary; both of them full of fine flour mingled with oil for a meat offering:*

2 ²⁰ One spoon of gold of ten shekels, full of incense:

3 ²¹ One young bullock, one ram, one lamb of the first year, for a burnt offering:

4 ²² One kid of the goats for a sin offering:

5 ²³ And for a sacrifice of peace offerings, two oxen, five rams, five he goats, five lambs of the first year: this was the offering of Nethaneel the son of Zuar.

6 *²⁴ On the **third day** Eliab the son of Helon, prince of the children of Zebulun, did offer:*

7 ²⁵ His offering was one silver charger, the weight whereof was an hundred and thirty shekels, one silver bowl of seventy shekels, after the shekel of the sanctuary; both of them full of fine flour mingled with oil for a meat offering:

The first tone is 396, the second tone is 417 and you just keep going down to verse 83 until you have all six tones. Notice that there are 6 repeating verses that go through 12 days, and that each tone is read from those matching verses. It is this repeating verse pattern that should alert people to the clue that there is encoded information hidden within these verses. In Numbers 7, the verses are almost like a puzzle that we have to figure out.

1. 396 Hz
2. 417 Hz
3. 528 Hz
4. 639 Hz
5. 741 Hz
6. 852 Hz

You should come up with the 6 frequencies that are listed above. Now when you focus on those 6 tones, a pattern should emerge. I noticed a pattern that I now call the wraparound effect. If you look at 396 Hz and 639 Hz, then you can see that the last number in 396 gets moved to the front of the number 639, so continue that pattern with all the numbers, and you will end up with 9 main Solfeggio tones.

1. 174 Hz
2. 285 Hz
3. 396 Hz
4. 417 Hz
5. 528 Hz
6. 639 Hz
7. 741 Hz
8. 852 Hz
9. 963 Hz

THE WRAPAROUND PATTERN OF THE SOLFEGGIO TONES

Revelation 22:13
I am Alpha and Omega, the beginning and the end, the first and the last.

9 TONE SCALE

1. 174 2. 285 3. 396

4. 417 5. 528 6. 639 The last number in the first row becomes the first number in the second row.

7. 741 8. 852 9. 963 The last number in the second row becomes the first number in the third row.

81 & 108 SKIP RATE

81

108 The zero is used as a placeholder when moving into the triple digits. The last number in the first row becomes the first number in the second row.

21, 102 & 210 SKIP RATE

21

102 The zero is used as a placeholder when moving into the triple digits. The last number in the first row becomes the first number in the second row.

210 The last number in the second row becomes the first number in the third row.

243, 324 & 432 SKIP RATE

243

324 The last number in the first row becomes the first number in the second row.

432 The last number in the second row becomes the first number in the third row.

The next pattern to recognize with the Solfeggio tones is that three of the numbers form a triad and belong together.

174 Hz 417 Hz 741 Hz
285 Hz 528 Hz 852 Hz
396 Hz 639 Hz 963 Hz

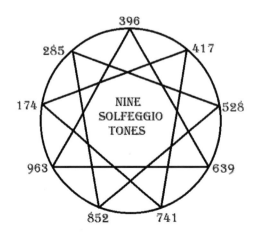

42

Many websites are putting the Solfeggio tones in a circle with three triangles to represent the triad of the three numbers. I did a graphic to show this relationship, and notice that this brings in the 153 triangle from our blueprint of the John 21 story. We can see that the triad of tones has a special relationship to the equilateral triangle. Now notice that these 9 tones do not form a Star of David or a hexagon. This means that this pattern is not yet complete, but I will show you step by step how to form the Star of David in the tones, and when we are complete there will be 4 Star of David patterns.

If you use Pythagorean math on the 9 tones, then you will find a 3, 6 and 9 pattern. Nikola Tesla once said, "If you only knew the magnificence of the 3, 6 and 9, then you would have a key to the universe."

Pythagorean Math   Skip Rates   Triplet Skip Rates

1) $1+7+4 = 12 = 1+2 = 3$ 174   174

-----------------------------------+111

2) $2+8+5 = 15 = 1+5 = 6$ 285   285

-----------------------------------+111   >243

3) $3+9+6 = 18 = 1+8 = 9$ 396   396

-----------------------------------+21   >243

4) $4+1+7 = 12 = 1+2 = 3$ 417   417

-----------------------------------+111   >243

5) $5+2+8 = 15 = 1+5 = 6$ 528   528   324

-----------------------------------+111   >324   -243

6) $6+3+9 = 18 = 1+8 = 9$ 639   639   **81**

-----------------------------------+102   >324

7) $7+4+1 = 12 = 1+2 = 3$ 741   741

-----------------------------------+111   >324

8) $8+5+2 = 15 = 1+5 = 6$ 852   852

-----------------------------------+111

9) $9+6+3 = 18 = 1+8 = 9$ 963   963

                                           102
                                           -21
                                           81

Looking at the spacing of the numbers, you can find patterns, which I call the skip rates of the tones. For example, 285-174 will give you the number 111, and this skip rate continues between 6 of the numbers. There is a definite pattern with the skip rates, and it also occurs between the skip rates of the triad numbers as well.

The next pattern that we are meant to notice is to continue the skip rate pattern that we see. In the skip rate pattern between the 9 tones, we can see 21 became 102. This is still the wraparound effect, but we see that a zero has become a placeholder to carry it into triple digits. The last number of 21 is placed in the front and a zero has been added. It is only logical at this point to carry on the wraparound effect to the third number. If we take the 2 at the end of 102 and place it in the front, then the next number becomes 210. This means that we can now go beyond the 9 main tones and bring them up to 12 tones. Ironically, this skip rate is also encoded in Numbers 7, so we can see that we are definitely meant to continue the skip rate pattern to find an additional 3 tones to add to our musical scale.

[13] And his offering was one silver charger, the weight thereof was an **hundred and thirty shekels**, *one silver bowl of* **seventy shekels**, *after the shekel of the sanctuary; both of them were full of fine flour mingled with oil for a meat offering:*

[14] One spoon of **ten shekels** *of gold, full of incense:*

The first hint of the 210 skip rate is given in verse 13 and 14. We are supposed to add the shekels together to help us to find the next tone in the series.

130 shekels + 70 shekels + 10 shekels= 210

The other skip rate pattern consist of the numbers 243 and 324, so again we are being presented with a very simple number pattern. We now need to use the wraparound effect to solve our puzzle.

243, 324, <u>432</u>

Okay, so now that we know what the skip rates are going to be in between the numbers, then it is just a matter of working out the last 3 numbers of this pattern.

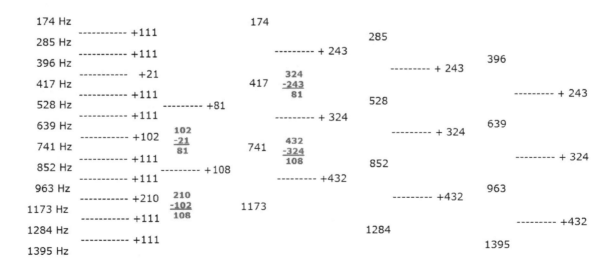

See how perfect the math works out between the Solfeggio tones, I like to call this beautiful math. It's flawless and perfect in every detail! Now notice that the numbers 81 and 108 come up in the skip rates. Remember the number 108 and its multiples come up all throughout the universe, and as I said in the first chapter, the sun's diameter is 108 times the Earth's diameter.

Also notice that the number 432 comes up in the triad skip rate. It's an interesting side note that all of the ancient instruments that have been found are tuned to the 432 Hz scale of music. I don't believe that it is a coincidence that this particular number also comes up in the Solfeggio tones. This number also connects with the 144 cubits measurement of the walls in New Jerusalem, and it connects with the 108 skip number. (432/3=144 108X4=432)

Another clue to the skip rate first shows up in verse 15, where it says, "**One** young bullock, **one** ram, **one** lamb of the first year, for a burnt offering:" We can clearly see that the 111 skip rate is hinted around in this verse and all of subsequent verses that follow.

Here is the clue to the purpose for the tones. In verse 17, it says "*And for a sacrifice of peace offerings, **two** oxen, **five** rams, **five** he goats, **five** lambs of the first year: this was the offering of Nahshon the son of Amminadab.*" Okay, so if we add the numbers in this verse, we will come up with the number 17 again, so we can clearly see a reference to the 153 fishing net of John 21. Isn't it ironic that the first verse that this clue is located in is verse number 17?

2 oxen + 5 rams + 5 goats + 5 lambs = 17

Now we are clearly being shown that the purpose for the tones is to make the fishing net of the harvest. By now though, you are probably wondering where the Star of David pattern in the net is located. I've shown you the equilateral triangles that the triad tones make, but I haven't shown you the other geometry that comes from these tones. This part of the puzzle is coming, but first I need to show you how to find the other tones because we are not yet finished.

Okay, now look at the first 12 tones and focus in on the 9 main tones. You might have already noticed that there are 3 more combinations that can be added to the triad numbers, so if you have you can go ahead and work these out. I discovered that there is another book in the Bible that contains the clues to these Solfeggio tones. The book of Psalms has 15 chapters that contain the Song of Degrees. The Song of Degrees starts at chapter 120 and continues through to chapter 135, and this song connects very well with the Solfeggio tones of Numbers 7. When I first started to read these chapters, I realized that the degrees that this song implied about in its title were referring to the 360 degrees of a circle. Once I understood that principle, I began to experiment with the degree circle more and apply some of the things that I had learned when I researched about Ed Leedskalnin's magnetic flywheel at Coral Castle in Homestead, FL. I broke up the degree circle into 15 degree intervals and started applying Pythagorean math to reduce the degrees to single digit integers. I also realized that the Song of Degrees began at chapter 120 for a reason, and I realized that a Perfect Star of David could be made within this circle starting at the 120 degrees position. I started a line at 120 degrees and drew it horizontal from the right to the left until it reached the 240 degree area of the circle and from there I continued drawing the lines until I had made a perfect Star of David within the degree circle. The angles on this Star of David are at a perfect 60 degree angle and both triangles are equilateral triangles.

Some interesting patterns started to emerge from the numbers that I was seeing, and I was able to see all of the triads that were associated with all of the 3, 6 and 9 numbers. Once I started to read only the triple digit numbers that were at the vertices of the hexagon or Star of David, I was able to come up with all of the various combinations of the 3, 6 and 9 numbers. Perhaps this is what Nikola Tesla discovered in his work with these numbers.

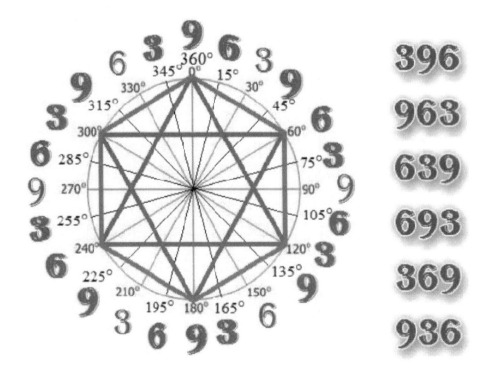

This is clear evidence that these tones are associated with the 360 degrees of a circle, and that the tones are also associated with the same geometrical shapes that the Bible teaches about in various stories or parables. It is only from reading these stories at a mathematical and scientific level that we have been able to uncover all of this encoded information. The interesting thing is that this degree circle seems to be associated with the city of New Jerusalem, which is mentioned in Revelation 21. If you use the 15 degree interval of the degree circle and the single digits of Pythagorean math, and then count all of the numbers going around the circle, then the sum will total to the number 144.

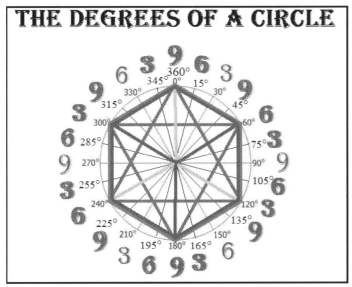

Revelation 21:17 *And he measured the wall thereof, an hundred and forty and four cubits, according to the measure of a man, that is, of the angel.* (angel/angle anagram)

Add all of the 3, 6 & 9's to get the number 144.

15° = 6	195° = 6
30° = 3	210° = 3
45° = 9	225° = 9
60° = 6	240° = 6
75° = 3	255° = 3
90° = 9	270° = 9
105° = 6	285° = 6
120° = 3	300° = 3
135° = 9	315° = 9
150° = 6	330° = 6
165° = 3	345° = 3
180° = 9	360° = 9

Some biblical scholars say that New Jerusalem is in the shape of a cube, and some say it is in the shape of a circle. We can see from this diagram that both are right, because within the degree circle there is a cube from a two dimensional perspective. In Rev. 21:17, it says *"And he measured the wall thereof, an **hundred and forty and four cubits**, according to the measure of a man, that is, of the angel."* We can see from the diagram that the 144 cubits does indeed "cube it" inside of the degree circle and the measure of an angel would be better understood as an anagram for the measure of an angle.

Now to find the other tones, we have to find all of the combinations to the triad numbers in the 9 main Solfeggio tones until we have all 9 of their counterparts, and then we continue the skip rate for these 9 tones to bring them up to 12 tones in this group as well. This will bring our total of

Solfeggio tones up to 24 tones altogether, and I will show you how these 24 tones connect with the 24 elders around the throne of God. You can look at the chart on the next page to find out if you got all of the 12 tones correctly. Notice that the skip rates of 102 and 21 have changed positions and that the 243 and 324 of the triad skip rates have also changed positions also.

THE OTHER 12 SOLFEGGIO TONES

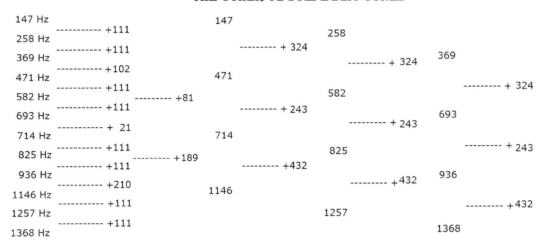

In Rev. 4:4, it says *"And round about the throne were **four and twenty seats**: and upon the seats I saw **four and twenty elders** sitting, clothed in white raiment; and they had on their heads crowns of gold"*. At some point in my research I realized that the 24 elders of Revelation 4 could be the 24 degrees around the degree circle with the 15 degree spacing. It also is the 24 Solfeggio tone scale. I took the 24 points or 15 degree intervals around the circle, and I decided to make Stars of David using those 24 points and to my surprise the 4 stars seemed to validate that the throne of God was indeed talking about this degree circle. Not only were the 24 elders the 24 points around the circle, but the four beasts seemed to be these 4 Stars of David that are made by connecting the 24 elders.

THE 24 POINTS ON A DEGREE CIRCLE

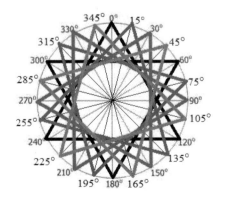

In Revelation 4:8, the verse says "*And the **four beasts had each of them six wings** about him; and they were full of eyes within: and they rest not day and night, saying, **Holy, holy, holy**, LORD God Almighty, which was, and is, and is to come*". We can see in the graphic above that the four beasts or Star of David's does have 6 wings or vertices on them. But you may ask, "what do these geometrical shapes of the Star of David have to do with the tones"? Well, remember there are 8 triads of tones that fit together and those triads form the triangles in the circle. The beast in the circle could be an anagram for beats, since we are talking about music. The beat in music is associated with a unit of time or the pulse, and it also can mean the rhythm or tempo of the song. I am not a musician or singer, so I can't completely understand the music concepts behind the mathematical concepts. Another clue that the four beasts are the stars is that in the mathematics of English gematria the word holy adds up to 60, and there are 60 degree angles in the vertices of the Star of David. An equilateral triangle is made up of three 60 degree angles, so Holy (60), Holy (60), Holy (60) makes up a triangle or a triad with the Solfeggio tones.

A=1	J=10	S=19
B=2	K=11	T=20
C=3	L=12	U=21
D=4	M=13	V=22
E=5	N=14	W=23
F=6	O=15	X=24
G=7	P=16	Y=25
H=8	Q=17	Z=26
I=9	R=18	

English Alphabet
Code

H=8 O=15 L=12 Y=25 (8+15+12+25=60)

As you can see there is a lot of geometry encoded into Revelation 4, and this song is a big part of that geometry. This encoded information shows us that there is a connection between geometry and music or sound. There is a science called Cymatics that shows the relationship between sound and geometry. Cymatics is the study of visible sound and vibration and it shows that all tones create specific geometrical shapes that are only unique to that tone. These geometrical shapes are like the fingerprints of music, as every human has their own unique fingerprint to them, likewise every sound or tone has a unique geometrical blueprint of their own. It's simply amazing!

In the Numbers 21 story, the Israelite people were being bitten by fiery serpents because of their sin, so the people asked Moses for help, and he prayed for them. In Numbers 21:8 "*the LORD said unto Moses, Make thee a fiery serpent, and set it upon a pole: and it shall come to pass, that every one that is bitten, when he looketh upon it, shall live*". Moses made a brass serpent and put it on the pole, and everyone that looked at it was healed of the serpent bites. Now here is where the story gets really interesting. After the serpent was placed on the pole, there are verses that talk about the Israelites pitching in many different places. Most people read this part from a literal interpretation and believe that the Israelites are merely pitching their tents, but there is another definition of pitching that seems to fit in better when take into account what happens after they did all of this pitching.

Numbers 21

*[10] And the children of Israel set forward, and **pitched** in Oboth.*

*[11] And they journeyed from Oboth, and **pitched** at Ijeabarim, in the wilderness which is before Moab, **toward the sunrising**.*

*[12] From thence they removed, and **pitched** in the valley of Zared.*

*[13] From thence they removed, and **pitched** on the other side of Arnon, which is in the wilderness that cometh out of the coasts of the Amorites: for Arnon is the border of Moab, between Moab and the Amorites.*

*[17] Then **Israel sang this song**, Spring up, **O well; sing ye unto it**:*

A musical pitch is a perceptual property that allows the ordering of sounds on a frequency related scale. The pitches can be defined as either higher or lower when associated with musical melodies. In this story the Israelites are pitching 4 times, so we can see a relationship between the four beast/beats around the throne of God and the Israelite pitching in a musical sense.

One of the times the Israelites are pitching east towards the rising sun, so perhaps this is a clue to the 4 points on a compass. Remember the compass was in with the net on the Bronze altar, so perhaps the four beasts are facing towards directions on a compass.

Exodus 27:5 *And thou shalt put it under the **compass** of the altar beneath, that the **net** may be even to the midst of the altar.*

In verse 17, the Israelites are singing a song, and we can see a relationship between this song and the net once again, because of the verse number.

Another interesting clue to the song that the Israelites sung is that they were singing to a well, which contains water. Fishing nets are always used inside of water, and it seems as if this song is supposed to be sung to water as well. This kind of reminds me of all the myths of mermaids that sing in the water to catch their fish. The baptism in the Old Testament was done in water, and this song appears to be used in conjunction with water, as well. If we are to use the hint of singing to a well and the hint of the verse number being a 153 net number, then it is fairly obvious that we must throw the net in the water to catch the fish.

In the book of Revelation there is a prophecy of 144,000 people from the 12 tribes of Israel that will sing a new song. We can now see that Numbers 21 also connects with this song and is prophetic of the Israelites singing a new song in the last days. It's interesting to me that a common symbol that is associated with music shows a staff with perhaps a snake going around the pole.

A clef is a musical symbol that is used to indicate the pitch of written notes, so perhaps it is somewhat ironic that it has to do with pitch and that turned upside down it sure looks like a shepherds staff or rod with a snake coiled around.

One day I was thinking about the triad tones in the Solfeggio and about how the 3, 6 and 9 patterns had a symbolic meaning to me of the 3 representing energy (it's an E backwards) and the 6 and 9 representing the yin/yang symbol. I realized that the triad of tones that creates triangles in the degree circle also represents the 3 forces within an atom. An atom has electrons that have a negative elementary electric charge, protons that have a positive charge and neutrons that are neutral. When I converted all of the Solfeggio tones into single digits using Pythagorean math to get the 3, 6 and 9 pattern, then I began to convert the tones into a positive, negative or neutral category. The threes are neutral, sixes are positive and nines are negative. When I was trying to figure which number of 6 or 9 represented which electrical charge, I finally decided that the number 9 has to represent the feminine, because after all the word femi**nine** has the word nine.

FIRST 12 TONES					SECOND 12 TONES	

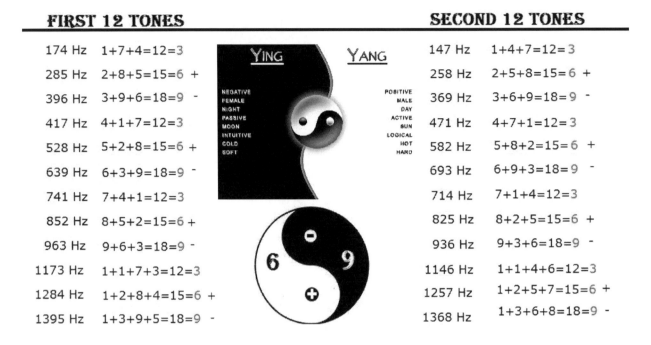

FIRST 12 TONES	SECOND 12 TONES
174 Hz 1+7+4=12=3	147 Hz 1+4+7=12=3
285 Hz 2+8+5=15=6 +	258 Hz 2+5+8=15=6 +
396 Hz 3+9+6=18=9 -	369 Hz 3+6+9=18=9 -
417 Hz 4+1+7=12=3	471 Hz 4+7+1=12=3
528 Hz 5+2+8=15=6 +	582 Hz 5+8+2=15=6 +
639 Hz 6+3+9=18=9 -	693 Hz 6+9+3=18=9 -
741 Hz 7+4+1=12=3	714 Hz 7+1+4=12=3
852 Hz 8+5+2=15=6 +	825 Hz 8+2+5=15=6 +
963 Hz 9+6+3=18=9 -	936 Hz 9+3+6=18=9 -
1173 Hz 1+1+7+3=12=3	1146 Hz 1+1+4+6=12=3
1284 Hz 1+2+8+4=15=6 +	1257 Hz 1+2+5+7=15=6 +
1395 Hz 1+3+9+5=18=9 -	1368 Hz 1+3+6+8=18=9 -

Now, let's see how the 9 main Solfeggio frequencies form into a cube. The "Emanation of the Solfeggio" paper written by Danny B Catselas Burisch Ph.D. and Marcia Ann McDowell, M.A. shows that the 9 Solfeggio frequencies can be displayed in a three dimensional configuration.

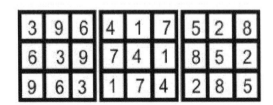

First you put all three frequencies that have the same numbers into a nine grid graph, and then you stack all three graphs to form a three dimensional cube. Notice that the nine Solfeggio frequencies are made up of 27 numbers that fit perfectly into a cube. The cube represents the Holy of Holies in the Tabernacle and the Temple, and it also represents the hexagon and Star of David from a two dimensional perspective. From a three dimensional perspective the cube represents the star tetrahedron, which is the energy pattern that is associated with the Merkaba or light chariot. The nine main tones are specifically meant to connect with the geometric cube to show us that listening to these tones puts us into a spiritual Holy of Holies.

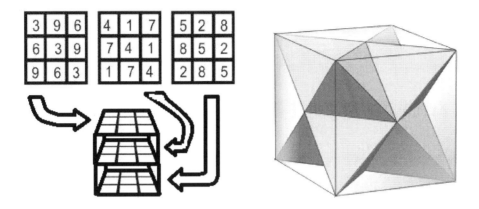

In Leviticus 23:27, the verse says *"Also on the tenth day of this seventh month there shall be a day of **atonement**: it shall be an holy convocation unto you; and ye shall afflict your souls, and offer an offering made by fire unto the LORD"*. The secret to the atonement is contained within the very word for those that have eyes to discern this words true meaning.

A-TONE-MENT

When listening to the Solfeggio tones, a human being is toning or tuning their body into God's frequency. This is very much like tuning into a radio station on a radio, only these higher frequencies tune you into a spiritual world in a higher dimension. Listening to the Solfeggio tones is like putting your body and soul on the Bronze Altar with the net and sitting in the fire of the Holy Spirit. You are the sacrifice on the altar, and the tones alter you, but the sacrifice that you are doing is one of sacrificing your will and replacing it with God's will. In Matthew 3:11 John the Baptist says, *"I indeed **baptize you with water** unto repentance. but he that cometh after me is mightier than I, whose shoes I am not worthy to bear: **he shall baptize you with the Holy Ghost, and with fire:"** Jesus revealed these tones in 1999, and these tones have been revealed in the Bible to be used on water. The Israelites sang to a well in Numbers 21 and the Apostles fished with the 153 net in the sea, so when the new song is sung by the 144,000 a net will be cast into this cosmic sea and the atonement of the whole Earth will begin.

The writers of the "Emanation of the Solfeggio" book also found out that 70% of the Solfeggio tones fall into the range of the colors red, blue and violet and only 30% fall into the color range of orange, green and yellow. The colors of the Solfeggio tones seem to represent the colors of a rainbow, and we know that God gave the rainbow to the Earth after the great flood. In the 9 main tones of the Solfeggio, the tone 528 Hz is in the color range of green, and this color is in the middle of the rainbow. I will cover more about the 7 primary colors in another chapter. It's interesting that 70% of the colors are in the red, blue and violet range, because those are the same colors that were used in the Tabernacle. In Exodus 26:1, it says "*Moreover thou shalt make the tabernacle with ten curtains of fine twined linen, and **blue**, and **purple**, and **scarlet**: with cherubims of cunning work shalt thou make them*". These colors represent the Phi proportion, which is also known as the Golden Ratio, Divine Proportion and it also contains the Fibonacci series of numbers,

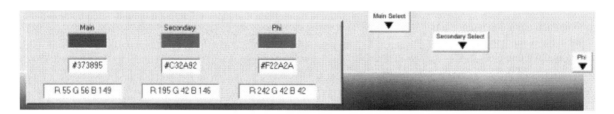

Every number in the Solfeggio scale is divisible by the number three. I have found so many connections with the number three in the Solfeggio tones, but one number turned out to be very close to the Phi number. I was trying to figure out if there were any patterns in the 21 and 102 skip numbers in the 9 main tones, and I accidently found a number that was so close to being Phi. This number is only off by 0.0010476, so dividing 21 into 102 gives us a multiple of Phi.

The 102 and 21

$102 - 21 = 81 / 3 = 27$
$102 + 21 = 123 / 3 = 41$
$102 \times 21 = 2142 / 3 = 714$ The 7th Tone on the 2nd Twelve Tones.
$102 / 21 = 4.8571428 / 3 = \mathbf{1.6190476}$ Approximates Phi

$$111 \quad 111 \quad \mathbf{21} \quad 111 \quad 111 \quad 102 \quad 111 \quad 111$$
$$/3 \quad /3 \quad /3 \quad /3 \quad /3 \quad /3 \quad /3 \quad /3$$
$$37 \quad 37 \quad 7 \quad 37 \quad 37 \quad \mathbf{34} \; 37 \quad 37 \quad \text{Prime Numbers}$$
$$\blacktriangledown$$
$$\text{(Even \#)}$$

DNA is 34 angstroms long and 21 angstroms wide.

The following graphic shows how every number in the Solfeggio scale is divisible by the number three, and even the skip rate numbers are divisible by three as well. Perhaps this is also showing us evidence for the trinity, because over and over the number three keeps being shown in all of the patterns. A triangle is made of 3 sides and has 3 vertices, and likewise all of the tones are in a triad together, and all of the tones are divisible by three.

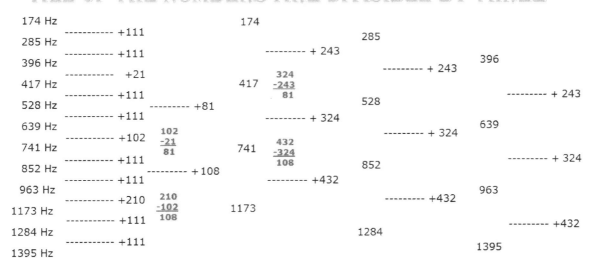

Solfeggio Tones: 174/3=58, 285/3=95, 396/3=132, 417/3=139, 528/3=176, 639/3=213, 741/3=247, 852/3=284, 963/3=321, 1173/3=391, 1284/3=428, 1395/3=465

Skip Rates: 111/3=37, 21/3=7, 102/3=34, 210/3=70, 81/3=27, 108/3=36, 243/3=81, 324/3=108, 432/3=144

I was looking at the first verses in Numbers 7 one day when two verses stood out to me as being peculiar. It seemed to be showing a number pattern, so I very quickly picked up on the hint to figure out the pattern and continue it beyond the 3 numbers presented.

Anytime we see a number pattern being presented to us, like we see in the Solfeggio tones, we are supposed to learn from it and complete the pattern. The Bible is meant to be an interactive workbook in which we not only read the Word of God, but we participate with it in an interactive way. We should recognize these patterns being presented to us, and not only that, but we should work out the math problems that are given to us and learn from them. The Bible is like a school textbook.

Numbers 7:7-8

[7] *Two wagons and four oxen he gave unto the sons of Gershon, according to their service:* [8] *And four wagons and eight oxen he gave unto the sons of Merari, according unto their service, under the hand of Ithamar the son of Aaron the priest.*

2,4,8..........

Now notice that each number doubles in this number pattern, so once you understand this pattern, then you can continue it on as far as you like. If you do continue the pattern, then you are likely to recognize certain numbers that come up, and particularly if you own a computer or work on one on your job. The numbers that come up are called binary byte numbers in the computer language, and it just means that every computer has memory storage or RAM chips that double in storage numbers. Most computers nowadays have 64 bit processors.

2,4,8,16,32,64,128,256,512,1024........

The number 64 has been found in our DNA. Our DNA has 64 codons, which are words in the genetic language. This number also comes up in I Ching, which is an ancient Chinese book. I Ching originated with Fu Xi, who said that the 8 trigrams were given to him supernaturally. The 8 trigrams each contain three lines, and each line is either "broken" or "unbroken," representing yin or yang, respectively. By the time of the legenday Yu, the trigrams had been developed into 64 hexagrams. Another interesting 64 connection is in the game of Chess, which has a board of 64 squares. Chess has probably originated in India, but no one knows for sure.

My stepdad, Kenny, looked at the pattern that I discovered in Numbers 7, and he said that these numbers also could trace our ancestry back in generations. We have 2 parents, 4 grandparents and 8 great grandparents etc., so these numbers also represent the numbering of past generations. It's interesting that the book of Numbers is teaching us some specific number patterns, and we should look at the title of the book as being a hint to the subject matter in some of its chapters.

The next thing that I noticed is that encoded within the Solfeggio tones is binary numbers, which is something else computer related that I never expected to find in the Bible. The interesting thing about binary numbers is that it is also a universal concept just like regular numbers. In other words, we could use binary code to communicate with an extraterrestrial race that would not be able to understand our language. In fact, binary code has already been used as a way to make contact with any extraterrestrial beings that encounter Earth's message. In 1972 binary code was used on the Pioneer 10 spacecraft and in 1974 it was transmitted into space as a message for ET's at Arecibo radio telescope in Puerto Rico. The Bible seems to be pointing out the binary code pattern, as well as the trinary code too. Binary uses the numbers 1 and 0 to establish patterns of true/false, yes/no, on/off etc. in computer programs, and trinary uses the numbers of 0,1 and

2. Notice in the graphic below how the binary number chart has a row of binary byte numbers above the 1's and 0's, and each column doubles from 2 to 4 to 8 to 16 to 32. This chart shows the relationship between binary byte numbers that are shown in Numbers 7:7-8 and the binary code that is shown in the Solfeggio tones math. Numbers 7 is teaching the concept of binary bytes and binary codes in the very same chapter.

TRINARY & BINARY CODE IN THE SOLFEGGIO TONES

174 Hz		147 Hz				
	---------- +111		---------- +111			
285 Hz		258 Hz				
	---------- +111		---------- +111			
396 Hz		369 Hz				
	---------- +21		---------- +102			
417 Hz		471 Hz				
	---------- +111		---------- +111			
528 Hz		582 Hz				
	---------- +111		---------- +111			
639 Hz		693 Hz				
	---------- +102		---------- +21			
741 Hz		714 Hz				
	---------- +111		---------- +111			
852 Hz		825 Hz				
	---------- +111		---------- +111			
963 Hz		936 Hz				
	---------- +210		---------- +210			
1173 Hz		1146 Hz				
	---------- +111		---------- +111			
1284 Hz		1257 Hz				
	---------- +111		---------- +111			
1395 Hz		1368 Hz				

Counting in Binary and Decimal

32	16	08	04	02	01		10	01
					1			1
				1	0			2
				1	1			3
			1	0	0			4
			1	0	1			5
			1	1	0			6
			1	1	1			7
		1	0	0	0			8
		1	0	0	1			9
		1	0	1	0		1	0
		1	0	1	1		1	1
		1	1	0	0		1	2
		1	1	0	1		1	3
		1	1	1	0		1	4
		1	1	1	1		1	5
	1	0	0	0	0		1	6

BINARY # 14

1110

258
285
528
582
825
+852
3330

3330/3=1110

TRINARY CODE

000 001 002
010 011 012   21=7
020 021 022

100 101 102
110 111 112   102=11
120 121 122

200 201 202
210 211 212   210=21
220 221 222

These numbers in Solfeggio math appear to be teaching us binary code, as well as trinary code.

In binary code the number 111 is equal to 7 and we know from Genesis 1 and 2 that the heavens and the Earth were created in 6 days, and God rested on the 7th day. This pattern was created within our calendar system of 7 days in a week. Also, the pattern of the Menorah in the Tabernacle and Temple has 7 candlesticks. It's quite obvious that God encoded the number 7 in the Solfeggio tones for a reason. I'll cover more about the 7 connection to our temple bodies in a chapter on electromagnetism, and this will show why the tones of the atonement are to be used for the remission of sins.

I was unable to cover all of the information that is included in the Solfeggio tones, but I will include some graphics of patterns I found in the appendix of this book. What amazes me is that after 8 years of studying them and listening to them, I am still from time to time finding more patterns and information that is encoded within these mysterious tones. It is like nothing that I have ever seen before, and I am convinced that somehow the entire universe is connected to these tones. This is God's music, and I have no doubt that there is still so much more information to discover within these tones.

We can now see that the pattern of God's Spirit on the face of the water is the same pattern of the number 153 in the John 21 story, and it is the same pattern in the Solfeggio tones. We can clearly see that the Bible contains the structure to the universe and the pattern being presented to us over and over again is being shown to reflect God's nature in an almost holographic way. I can't help but think of a quote from the Gospel of Thomas that says "Split a piece of wood, and I am there. Lift up the stone, and you will find me there." The pattern being presented to us is showing us a pattern that can be found in the microscopic universe as well as the macroscopic universe, so this same energetic pattern repeats at different levels of perception. Its interesting that the Star of David is written into this pattern, because the two triangles point up and down and its principle reflects the old hermetic saying of "As above, so below". I can't think of any better saying that reflects the nature of God's Creation.

Astronomy in the Bible

Genesis 1:14 And God said, Let there be lights in the firmament of the heaven to divide the day from the night; and let them be for signs, and for seasons, and for days, and years:

In the verse above, there is little doubt that those lights are from the sun, the moon and the stars. The orbit around our sun measures one year, the moon's orbit around the earth measures about a month and the Earth's rotation on its axis measures one day. Most people don't look to the star constellations as another measure of time, but the 12 zodiac constellations create a very long calendar that measures the precession of the equinoxes cycle. That cycle last for 25,920 years and is divided by 12 ages lasting 2,160 years each. The Earth has a slight wobble which causes it to trace out a big circle in the sky during one precession cycle, and it points towards the 12 zodiac constellations while it is moving along. Each age of 2,160 years is named for the constellation that the Earth is pointing towards during that time period. We have just completed the Age of Pisces, and we are now in the Age of Aquarius. You can view this wobble circle as being similar to a big gigantic clock and each hour would be equal to an age on that precession clock.

The Bible does a very good job of teaching about the precession of the equinoxes, but most people fail to catch on to what the pattern of the Tabernacle and other clues in the Bible are showing us about this cycle of time. I happened to stumble upon this idea when I was researching about the Tabernacle, because I began to question why the incense and bronze altar had 4 horns. It didn't make any sense to me about why there had to be horns. Suddenly one day I was looking at the constellations and somehow it popped into my head that perhaps two of those horns represented the horns of Taurus. I was writing a book about the Israelites' connection to Taurus and about the Exodus route tracing out Taurus in the Sinai Peninsula, so it made sense to me that this idea might work out. I began to check the other constellations in the precession to see if the next constellation had horns as well, and the next constellation was Aries, which is a Ram with horns. I checked the next constellation to see what it was and if perhaps it would match up somehow, and it did too. The next two furniture stands in the Tabernacle are the table of shewbread and the Menorah, so it has two objects in the same area, and they seemed to match Pisces which represents two fish. The next object is the bronze water laver, and it was located just outside of the Tabernacle, so I checked to see what constellation was next, and it was Aquarius. That fit perfectly too, because Aquarius is the water bearer, so it seemed obvious that a water laver would be symbolic of that constellation. The next pattern of the bronze altar threw me for a loop, because Capricorn and Sagittarius didn't fit the pattern. Capricorn has horns, but Sagittarius does not, so I realized that the bronze altar and the incense altar represented the same two constellations.....they are the exact same pattern. It seemed obvious to me that both of them were representing the same two constellations.

The Tabernacle Star Map

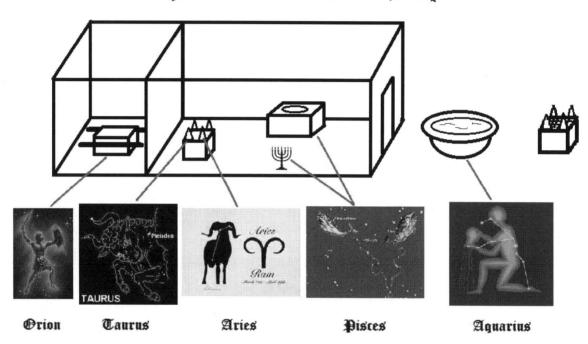

Orion   Taurus   Aries   Pisces   Aquarius

Once I discovered this star map, I wanted to see if anyone else had found the pattern to be a star map too. I couldn't find anything for a long while, but then I found one website that had the information that I was looking for on the net. I found what I was looking for to corroborate my theory that the Tabernacle pattern was indeed a star map, and that some Jewish rabbis had known of this star map. In the Zohar, it said that the Tabernacle corresponds to the structure of heaven and earth, and that it was made after the pattern of the supernal. One definition of the word supernal is "of or relating to the sky or the heavens; celestial".

- **Soncino Zohar, Shemoth, Section 2, Page 149a - "... the structure of the Tabernacle corresponds to the structure of heaven and earth."**
- **Soncino Zohar, Shemoth, Section 2, Page 231a - "Now, the Tabernacle below was likewise made after the pattern of the supernal Tabernacle in all its details. For the Tabernacle in all its works embraced all the works and achievements of the upper world and the lower, whereby the Shekinah was made to**

abide in the world, both in the higher spheres and the lower. Similarly, the Lower Paradise is made after the pattern of the Upper Paradise, and the latter contains all the varieties of forms and images to be found in the former. Hence the work of the Tabernacle, and that of heaven and earth, come under one and the same mystery."

Another exceptional detail of the pattern is that it also is a calendar as well. Orion is not a constellation in the precession of the equinoxes, but all of the other constellations are in the zodiac. Taurus represents the Age of Taurus, Aries represents the Age of Aries, Pisces represents the Age of Pisces and Aquarius represents our present Age of Aquarius. Not only was this pattern meant to be a star map, but it was meant to show us a timeline as well. According to biblical scholars, Adam and Eve were placed in the Garden of Eden about 6,000 years ago and this would have been during the Age of Taurus. The Age of Taurus started approximately 6,480 years ago, and lasted for 2,160 years, and this is the timeframe of Adam and Eve, the tower of Babel and the great flood etc. The Age of Aries was about 4320 years ago, and this was the time period of the slavery of the Israelites in Egypt and the time of the Exodus. The next age was the Age of Pisces, which started 2,160 years ago, and it was during this age that Jesus Christ was born into this world. We can see that three precession ages have gone by in this supernal clock, and now we have recently started into the Age of Aquarius. The timeline ends at this age, so we see that the Tabernacle has only one third of the precession star constellations, and these 4 ages represent a total of 8640 years. Two of the skip rates that come up in the Solfeggio tones also correlate with the precession of the equinox numbers. The numbers 108 and 432 divides evenly into 8640, as well as the 144 cubits of New Jerusalem.

$$8640/108=80 \quad 8640/144=60 \quad 8640/432=20$$

The sun has a diameter of 864,000 miles, so 8640 is a divisor of that number. It's interesting that the 144 number from Revelation 21 is in the degree circle math and is a multiple of 8640. The number 144 in the Bible is a precession of the equinox number. The Earth moves 1 degree every 72 years, and it moves 2 degrees every 144 years. The Bible is trying to show us this precession cycle in the Tabernacle star map and the Song of Degrees math. It's interesting that the star map ends at the Age of Aquarius. Why didn't the pattern show the complete 12 precession constellations? Is something going to happen during the Age of Aquarius? These are questions that we should be thinking about when viewing this encoded information. The number 144 is only mentioned in Revelation 21, but as I have shown you the number 144 came up in the 15 degree intervals of the degree circle and the number 144 comes up in the precession of the equinoxes. Remember the Earth's wobble traces out a circle, and this circle has 360 degrees, so the Song of Degrees that contains the 3, 6 and 9 Solfeggio tones also reveals the precession of the equinoxes. We can see clear connections between the Song of Degrees, the Solfeggio tones and the Tabernacle pattern.....they all relate to precession of the equinoxes.

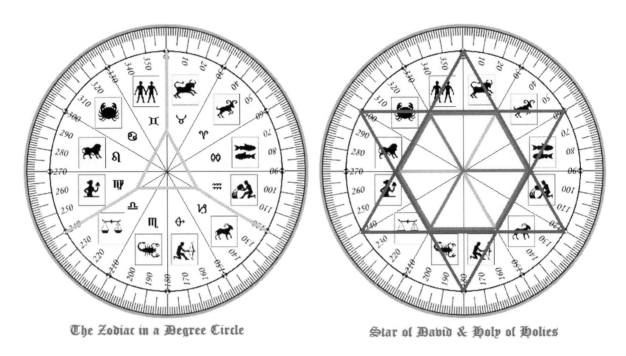

The Zodiac in a Degree Circle   Star of David & Holy of Holies

The same pattern that we have been following all along repeats again in the precession of equinox map in the Tabernacle. It only shows 4 ages of precession in the Tabernacle pattern, so if we look at the zodiac in the degree circle we will find some more connections. I transferred the zodiac to the degree circle, and I started the Age of Taurus at 0 degrees and looked for where the 4th age ends. The 4th age ends at 120 degrees, and this is where a perfect Star of David can be drawn out within the degree circle. The triangle in the first graphic shows that the Bible gave us 1/3 of the precession constellations, which gives us the key to tracing out the Star of David at 0 and 120 degrees, which makes up one side of the equilateral triangle. The 2nd graphic shows the Star of David clue drawn out inside of a degree circle, and it also shows the Holy of Holies cube.

In the book "The astral origin of the emblems, the zodiacal signs, and the astral Hebrew Alphabet", Rev. J. H. Broome compares the Hebrew letters to the star constellations. The Hebrew alphabet starts with the Alef letter, and that letter just happens to represent the constellation of Taurus. Over and over again, we keep seeing the same pattern of Taurus as being very significant to the Jewish people.

I realized that the constellations on the tabernacle star map could be converted into Hebrew letters, so I took the chart and started to match each letter with its constellation. The letters didn't seem to form a word, so I turned my attention next to the numbers of those letters, and this is where I found another hidden message within the tabernacle.

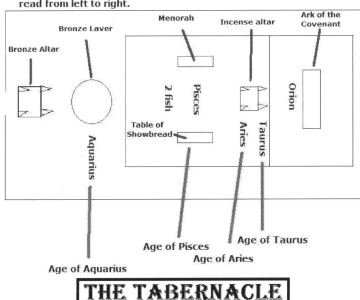

I aligned it the opposite way then it is in the sky, so that it could be read from left to right.

THE TABERNACLE
Star map & Timeline

The constellations in the tabernacle star map can be converted into Hebrew numbers.

לאיבלאע

I removed the Orion number, because it is in the Holy of Holies cube and is not a part of the timeline. I got six numbers, which I immediately knew were latitude and longitude coordinates. I had to read the numbers backwards, because Hebrew is read from right to left. Here are the coordinates.

30 1 10 / 2 30 1
or
+30° 1' 10.00", +2° 30' 1.00

The coordinates mark an area in Algeria, Africa. What is there? Nothing, but a road named N51. (51X3=153) Read John 21 in your Bible.

There are seven numbers in the tabernacle star map, the first one starts with Aries. Hebrew is read from right to left, and so I had to read it from the Bronze Altar to Orion, which turns it upside down from the way it is in the sky. Orion is located in the Holy of Holies cube, and it is the last number on the star map, the letter for Orion is Tsadeh and its number is 90. The number 90 in geometry represents a right angle of 90 degrees, and that fits in perfect with its position. The Holy of Holies is in the shape of a cube, and we all know that a cube is made up of right angles.

The first six numbers represent the timeline, and I realized that I should keep them separate from Orion. That was when I realized that the six numbers could be latitude and longitude numbers. Aries is the last constellation in the star map, but its number is read first in the Hebrew language.

When I was converting the Hebrew letters into numbers, I made a mistake when I looked at the number for the letter for Pisces. I had mistaken Bet for Kaf because they both looked exactly alike, and I then went on to locate the coordinates. Later on, I realized my mistake and replaced the number 2 for Pisces with the number 20, and then I looked for the coordinates, only to find that they weren't significant. I looked at the letter Bet and Kaf and realized how closely they resembled one another, and then I thought maybe it wasn't my mistake, but perhaps it was a mistake made by Rev. J. H. Broome. The Hebrew letter for Pisces could very easily be the letter that he assigned to the constellation of Gemini. I decided to go with my intuition and follow my first choice. The letter for Pisces is Bet in my opinion, so that is a change that I have made to J. H. Broome's chart.

The star constellations, letters, and numbers are listed below.

1. Aries is the letter Lamed and is the number 30.

2. Taurus is the letter Alef and is the number 1.

3. Aquarius is the letter Yud and is the number 10.

4. Pisces is the letter Bet and is the number 2.

5. Aries is the letter Lamed and is the number 30.

6. Taurus is the letter Alef and is the number 1.

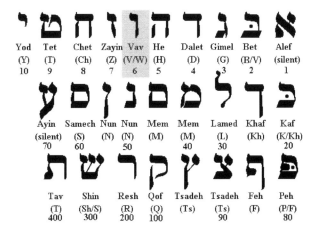

The latitude and longitude coordinates are positioned within the country of Algeria in Africa, and there appears to be nothing in this location. There is a road that goes through the area that has been numbered as N51. Isn't it interesting that a 153 divisor comes up at this location?

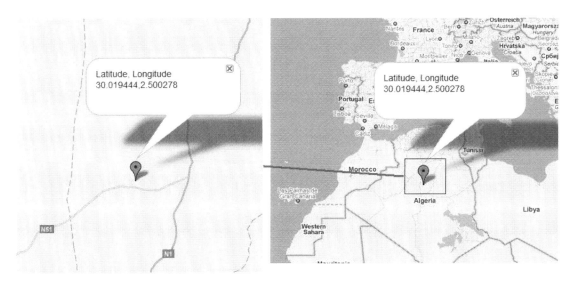

The N51 road is a clue, but a clue to what? Well, that stumped me quite a bit at first, and I thought that some organization must have already found whatever was buried there. I knew that I couldn't have been the only one to find the latitude and longitude coordinates of the tabernacle. Then I noticed something rather significant, as I turned my gaze northward. This position was directly under France, and that was when my research from past projects started to converge into one massive project. I just couldn't believe what I was seeing. I was ecstatic with enthusiasm because for the first time on my journey of discovery, I was starting to understand how all of the puzzle pieces were starting to fit together into one gigantic puzzle. The Basque people are generally looked upon as being the origins for the rare RH negative blood type, and they live in France and Spain. Approximately 35% of the Basque people have RH negative blood types and nearly 60% have RH negative alleles. The Berber Tribe that lives in northern Africa also carries a higher percentage of RH negative blood, and many people believe that either the Berbers migrated from the Basques lands or vice versa. Either way, the area that the coordinates marks is a hot zone of RH negative people.

When I drew a line straight up from the coordinates, then I realized that this arrow would go right through the Pyrenees Mountains of France, and this is the area that the Basque live and near the area that Mary Magdalene came to live in France.

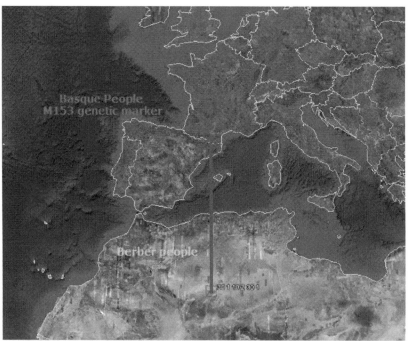

This area is a hot zone for RH negative blood. The Basque people are the origin for this bloodline, and they have the most RH negative of any people on the Earth. It is theorized by many that the Berber people migrated from the Basque.

As I mentioned before, an interesting parallel to the John 21 story has to do with the number that geneticists have given to the Basque genetic marker. That number is M153. Why would the geneticists give the Basque genetic marker that particular number? If some organization or government has tied the Basque people to Jesus, then it was obvious to me that the grail theory that Jesus Christ and Mary Magdalene were married seemed to fit perfectly.

Could the coordinates have marked the area that a new bloodline would be started? That is a definite possibility, but also there could be another reason to mark the area of France. Another interesting detail about France is that it is often referred to as the L'Hexagone or the hexagon, and the hexagon is associated with the Star of David and the Holy of Holies cube. This would, of course, connect France with the Jews, and so does the grail race legends of France.

The shape of France is not a perfect hexagon, but it matches very closely to the Winter Hexagon in the sky. When I realized that France could represent the Winter Hexagon in the sky, then I automatically saw the connection to the tabernacle star map. The Winter Hexagon consists of 6 constellations that can be linked together to form an irregular hexagon shape. Two of those constellations are in the tabernacle star map, and they are Orion and Taurus. It is interesting to me that Mary Magdalene ended up moving to the country of France.

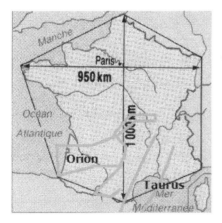 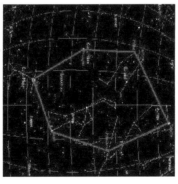 

Winter Hexagon

A few months ago I was exploring the Roseline or Paris meridian when I was doing some research about Mount Hermon. I realized that Mount Sion in the Bible was actually Mount Hermon after I looked up the word Sion on Bible Gateway. In Deuteronomy 4:48 it says, *"From Aroer, which is by the bank of the river Arnon, even unto **mount Sion, which is Hermon**"*. I never realized that Mount Sion and Mount Zion were two different places until I read that verse. What is interesting about the Roseline or Paris meridian is that Mount Hermon is exactly 33.33 degrees north latitude and 33.33

degrees east longitude. Jesus Christ was crucified at the age of 33 years old, and Mount Hermon is said to be the mountain that Jesus may have transfigured on, because he was preaching in the area just days before this happened. This also links to the 144,000 and the new song. In Revelation 14:1 the verse says *"And I looked, and, lo, a Lamb stood on the **mount Sion**, and **with him an hundred forty and four thousand**, having his Father's name written in their foreheads"*. As I've mentioned before all of the Solfeggio tones and the skip rates are divisible by three, so 33.33 seems like a lot of clues all wrapped up in one.

The Roseline in myth is associated with the Grail bloodline, which are said to be descendants of Jesus Christ and Mary Magdalene. This name comes from one verse in the Bible. In Song of Solomon 2:1 the verse says, *"I am the rose of Sharon, and the lily of the valleys"*. People debate as to whether the rose is talking about the groom or the bride. The Song of Solomon is said by many to be prophetic of Jesus Christ, and the church and that it is referring to the marriage of the Lamb that is referred to in the book of Revelation. Some say the rose of Sharon is referring to Jesus and some say that it is referring to his bride, which is the church. In Isaiah **35:1**, it says, *"The wilderness and the solitary place shall be glad for them; and the desert shall rejoice, and blossom as the rose"*. This verse is referring to Israel being restored, so we can see that the rose of Sharon could be referring to the bride. Another interpretation in the Grail legends is that Mary Magdalene is the rose, since she was said to be the bride of Jesus. I find it interesting that the chapter and verse numbers in Isaiah seem to reflect the 153 net that was tossed into Iberia, because like a reflection on the sea the number 153 is in reverse. Perhaps we can envision the Tabernacle at the latitude and longitude coordinates casting out the net on the bronze altar into the Mediterranean Sea just above Algeria and then releasing the fish into Iberia. From the Tabernacle coordinates site we see nothing but the desert, but the line drawn upward from the site is like a thorny stem that grew into a rose in France. It's ironic that Mary Magdalene according to legends came to France in a boat from the Mediterranean Sea. Perhaps the net caught the fish in the east just as John 21 says, because Israel is to the east of the Mediterranean Sea. The Israelites were then transplanted to the Iberia area and the grail bloodline began.

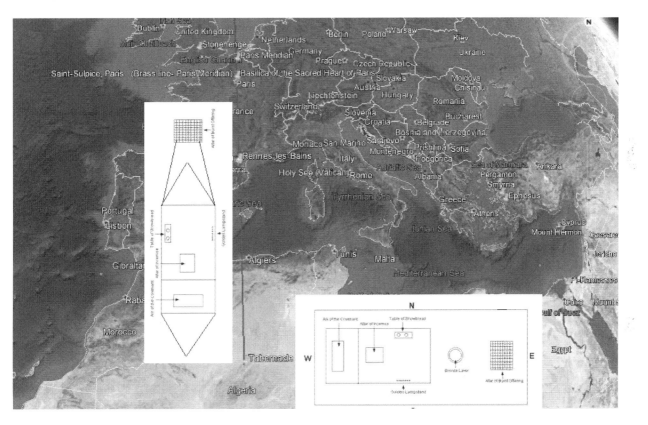

There are other astronomy clues that are hidden within the Bible. The Bible especially talks about Orion, the Pleiades and Arcturus in Job. In **Job 9:9, it says** "*Which maketh Arcturus, Orion, and Pleiades, and the chambers of the south.* Orion is in the Holy of Holies in the star map and the Pleiades is a star group of 7 main stars that is located in the constellation to Taurus. The Pleiades is inside of the incense and the bronze altar in the star map. There is a special verse that tells us to look at a specific area of the sky. In Job 38:31 it says, "Canst thou bind the sweet influences of **Pleiades**, or loose the bands of **Orion**? If we look in this section of the sky, then we should notice that in between Orion and the Pleiades are the horns of Taurus. I discovered that there is a very interesting star located inside the horns of Taurus. I wondered if the Bible could have been giving us a clue here, and when I wrote the book "The Cosmic Lighthouse" I put forth a theory that the Bible is indeed giving us a clue to find an interesting anomaly found in the horns of Taurus.

The Bible poses a curious question to the reader, and it almost seems like a riddle to me. The first thing that we should be thinking when we read Job 38:31 is about the location of Orion and the Pleiades in the sky. The Bible is hinting around about this area for a reason, and we must figure out why. In fact the whole chapter of Job 38 is trying to get us to think about its verses and not only that, but the Bible is trying to get us to research its content and to ponder the answers to its riddles. This is definitely an interactive chapter!

Job 38

30 The waters are hid as with a stone, and the face of the deep is frozen.

31 Canst thou bind the sweet influences of Pleiades, or loose the bands of Orion?

This is the same chapter that had us looking and pondering over the meaning of a snowflake, and it had us looking at the face of water that is frozen. What is fascinating is that the question about the Pleiades and Orion is put right under the water crystal hint. Orion is located in the Holy of Holies in the Tabernacle star map, and the HOH was cube shaped, so we have an interesting connection to the hexagonal water crystal. Another connection can also be found in the body of Orion, not only is his body shaped like an hourglass, but it is also an odd 6 sided hexagon shape. It certainly can't be a coincidence that these two verses were put next to one another, because we can see that the lesson of the hexagonal water crystal carries over to the Holy of Holies cube that Orion is located within the inside of the Tabernacle star map.

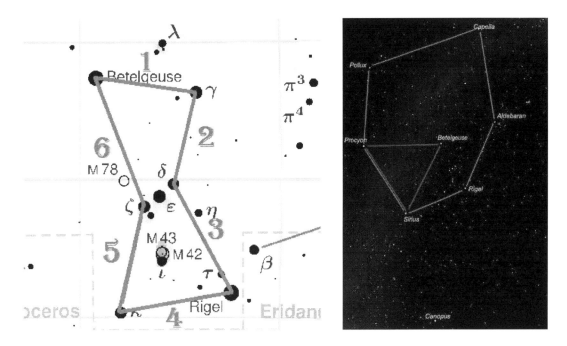

Not only is Orion hexagonal in shape, but an asterism that Orion belongs within is called the Winter Hexagon. It consists of 6 stars forming an imperfect hexagon shape, and one is in Orion and another is in Taurus. The Winter Triangle is also located within this hexagon, and it is a perfect equilateral triangle.

Now, let's get back to the hint to look at the horns of Taurus, which are located in between Orion and the Pleiades. Years ago I read a book by Paul A. LaViolette called "Decoding the Message of the Pulsars". In this book, he tells about three special pulsars that are extremely unique to our Milky Way galaxy. Inside the horns of Taurus is the Crab Nebula and the Crab pulsar, and this pulsar is the most luminous pulsar in the sky. The Crab pulsar emits pulses in the radio frequencies, optical, X-ray and Gamma rays. It ranks as being the fourth brightest when measured in radio frequencies. The Crab pulsar is among the rare 1% of pulsars that produces a secondary pulse that occurs midway in between the main pulses and so it is called a millisecond pulsar. The Crab pulsar has a period of 33.4 milliseconds, and that was the exact age of Jesus Christ at the time of his crucifixion. This pulsar is slowly speeding up to 34 milliseconds, and this is a Fibonacci number and this is quite unusual among pulsars. Most pulsars are gradually slowing down over time, but out of the 1,533 pulsars, there is a subset of just 24 pulsars that are speeding up. I find it really interesting that the number 1,533 seems to echo the 153 fish of John 21 and the number 24 is mentioned in Revelation 4 as being the elders around the throne of God and is the number of Solfeggio tones in the special group that I found. Sure this could be a coincidence, but one of those 24 pulsars is located where the Bible hinted around for us to look in the sky. By the way, pulsars could only be found in our modern days with huge radio telescopes, so there is no way that these questions in the Bible could have been answered in the ancient past. These questions and riddles seem to be directed entirely to our modern day generations.

There are two other pulsars that match up in a line with the Crab pulsar, and they are just as unique. The Vela pulsar is the brightest radio frequency pulsar in the sky, and it outshines the other pulsars by several hundred times. Like the Crab pulsar, Vela emits pulses in the radio frequencies, optical, X-ray and Gamma rays. The Crab and the Vela pulsars are the only known pulsars that pulse in these four spectral regions of the electromagnetic scale. The Vela pulsar also belongs to the 1% of the millisecond pulsars, and its rotational period is 89.3 milliseconds. Ironically enough, Vela's period is a Fibonacci number.

The Vulpecula doesn't have the same features as the Crab and Vela pulsars, but it is aligned with them. Its distinctive feature is that it is located only 0.13 degrees from the Galactic center's one radian longitude meridian which is closer than any other pulsar. The period of Vulpecula is 144.4 milliseconds.

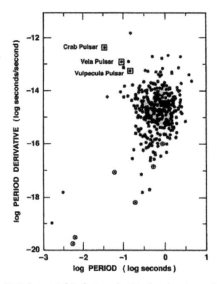

Figure 37. Pulsar period P (horizontal axis) plotted against pulsar period derivative P (vertical axis) on a logarithmic graph for 305 pulsars (after Dewey, et al., Astrophysical Journal, figure 2b). The squares mark the coordinates for the Crab, Vela, and Vulpecula pulsars.

These three stars are aligned to the galactic equator, and all of them are in areas of supernova remnants. LaViolette believes that these three special pulsars are warnings of a galactic core explosion because they mark areas that show evidence of the last galactic core explosion that happened in the Milky Way galaxy. The Crab pulsar is speeding up to 34 milliseconds, the

Vela is 89 milliseconds and Vulpecula is 144 milliseconds, so all of these numbers are displaying the Fibonacci sequence of numbers, which are also associated with the Phi spiral or Golden spiral.

The Fibonacci Sequence

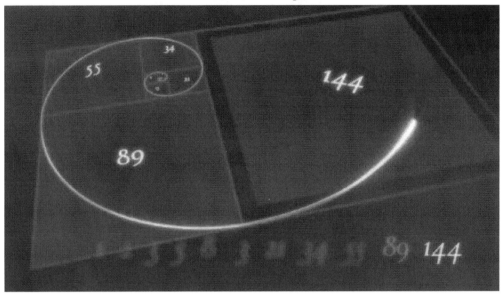

0, 1, 1, 2, 3, 5, 8, 13, 21, **34**, 55, **89**, **144**.....

Vulpecula's period reminds me of the measurements of the walls of New Jerusalem that are 144 cubits, which is mentioned in Rev. 21:17. An interesting connection that is encoded in this verse shows a parallel between the numbers 144 and 153. The verse number is at 17, which we know is associated with the number 153. The connection between these two numbers has a 9 pattern. If we add the digits together for both numbers, we will get the number 9, and if we subtract 144 from 153 we will get 9, also both numbers are multiples of the number 9. I will be covering more about number pattern in another chapter.

$$1+4+4=9$$

$$1+5+3=9$$

$$153-144=9$$

$$144/9=16 \quad 153/9=17$$

It's interesting that the Bible is giving us astronomy clues to precession of the equinox, the Fibonacci number sequence, a timeline or astronomical calendar and showing us some special pulsars to possibly warn us of a galactic core explosion. The Bible shows us that our galaxy and the Earth are intricately connected, and that we can measure time by the movement of the wobble of the Earth. This anomaly of just a slight wobble in the Earth's movement might not be by accident, but by Divine design, and the Tabernacle pattern that teaches us this galactic calendar is a gift by the greatest architect of both time and space. The stars speak to us in unimaginable ways, and they display the beauty of God's grand design, because like lighthouses guide the sailors on the sea and warn them about the dangers ahead, God's light in the stars above guide us through space and time. God told us that the lights in the night sky would be for signs, seasons, days and years. The Architect of our universe displays His wisdom from the tiniest atom to the cells in our bodies and to the stars in the sky, and at every level from the microscopic to the macroscopic, we can see the patterns are always the same. The Bible displays the scientific and mathematical truths to His creation, but only if we know how to read them and where to look.

DNA: THE BOOK OF LIFE

Revelation 20:12 And I saw the dead, small and great, stand before God; and the books were opened: and another book was opened, which is the book of life: and the dead were judged out of those things which were written in the books, according to their works.

Last year I got a DNA test done to see where my ancestors came from, and this test surprised me with some of the answers I received. My DNA had literally spoken to me and it was able to tell me where 1,000 years of my past generations had lived. It has only been in our modern times that we have been able to open up this book of life and to look at the secrets that it holds from within the microcosm of inner space. I still remember when I first watched the PBS series called Cosmos, and there was an episode where Carl Sagan talks about inner space and the DNA. He said that 5 billion bits of information are contained within our DNA, and that all of the information could be put into about 1,000 volumes of books in a library. At that time I was just in the eighth grade, and I couldn't wrap my head around how something so tiny that can't even be seen with our eyes could contain so much information. This was before our small computers of today and before the tiny SD cards that holds anywhere from 2 gigabytes to 64 gigabytes of data, but even then in our present time I still can't even imagine how our microscopic DNA can hold so much information. Mankind can't even begin to compete with God's creation, and even our brain is so much more advanced than our modern day computers. Imagine a whole world on the top of a pin, and you would be getting close to the majesty of God's kingdom, which is so infinitely complex that we can't even begin to imagine it in all of its splendor. There are so many more levels to reality that exists, and we can't even begin to contemplate it all in all of its splendid glory. My body consists of little tiny spirals of DNA that hold the very blueprints of all that I am and each DNA strand within every microscopic cell of my body has a library of data at the nucleus of thousands of cells. All of this is within me, but I can't even experience it from my present perspective. It's weird to think that a lot of who I am can't even be seen in the physical world, because it is an invisible part of who I am. It's incredible to contemplate that most of who we are in the physical world is unseen, and from the microscopic level to the atomic level we exist in a world that is completely not experienced by our conscious self. Go even further down into whom we are, and you would see the tiniest atom which seems to reflect the macrocosm of a solar system. Zoom out to the level of our physical universe of matter, and the universe becomes a very big place that we can't even begin to imagine as it almost seems to go out into infinity and beyond. Physicists now tell us that there are other dimensions of space that we can't even see nor can we explore. We think we know reality, but the unfathomable truth is that we know very little about reality as a whole. We only see and experience just a fraction of what our reality really consists of in this world.

In Revelation 20:12, we are told that God will judge us based on what is written in the book of life. In 1953, Francis Crick and James D. Watson discovered the spiraling DNA, and very shortly after the phrase "book of life" was used to describe this microscopic blueprint for our bodies. Now a little over 50 years later, we are being told that scientists have only been able to decipher 3% of what the DNA does, and that the rest of the DNA contains junk code that is no longer applicable to our lives. This certainly is a conundrum of modern day genetics when they can only determine that 3% of our DNA has a function inside of our bodies. Imagine picking up a book to read only to find out that 3% of it is in English and the rest of it is in a completely unrecognizable language, and so in frustration you are unable to read the rest of the book. Would you simply dismiss the problem because the rest of the book must be nothing important? This is what the geneticists have done, because they were unable to come up with a purpose for the rest of the DNA. Just because they can't find a physical purpose for 97% of DNA code does not mean that there isn't one. In Rev. 20:12, we are told very clearly another purpose for the book of life, only this purpose is not of a physical nature but of a spiritual one. Could it be that the book of life doesn't just merely tell how we are made, but that it also tells about the life that we have lived? The Bible suggests that the DNA could actually be recording the details of our very lives in much the same way that a VCR, DVD recorder or a DVR records the television programs that we want to watch later on when we have more time.

Furthermore, there is empirical proof that this is to be the case. There have been many books written about the near death experience in which they describe the events that took place following their own death. In all cases the people described their soul as leaving their physical body and then some of them were pulled into or attracted towards a tunnel or black hole. After these souls came out of the tunnel, they came into a world of light, and they had to go through a life review, which they all describe as being a three dimensional projection of all of their memories being displayed before them. In all of the cases that I have read of the life review, they said that not only were they seeing and experiencing all of their memories, but that they were able to feel the consequences of their actions by being able to feel how it made the others around them feel. They were actually being able to judge their own lives, and many would say that they would feel ashamed when they did something that hurt someone else. The purpose of them watching their life review did not seem to be one of punishment, but it was just being used to help the soul to learn more about the consequences of their actions. The NDE's description of the life review certainly makes me think about this scripture that says we will be judged out of the book of life, and it adds to the evidence that perhaps our lives are recorded from the book of life we call our DNA.

When the book of Revelation was written, no one could have ever understood what this book of life could possibly be. Perhaps the ancient readers of this book merely pictured a scroll in their mind as they read this verse, and maybe people of the Middle Ages and beyond have pictured a bound book like we have today. No one in the past could have ever imagined that one day human beings would be able to know what this book looks like and how it works. Nor would they have ever imagined that mankind would be able to open this book and to actually discover what 3% of it can do. It is perhaps a shock to our modern days that the Lamb's book of life is microscopic and unable to be seen with the naked eye. It is inconceivable to even begin to understand the complexities of how such a tiny structure is able to help make our physical bodies and perhaps record everything that happens within our lives, but nevertheless the Bible and NDE's show us that this could be true.

We are told in Matthew 10:30 that the hairs of our head are all numbered, and that information would be stored in the DNA. Genetic tests are being done to show the maternal and paternal parents of someone. They are being done in criminal trials now to prove innocence or guilt; they are being done to show where our ancestors once lived; they are being done to show if Europeans or Asians have any Neanderthal DNA, and they are being done to show if we have any genetic abnormalities that will lead to diseases. Within our book of life all of these answers can be found, and it is the key to unlocking many secrets. Our genetics are incapable of lying, and so within this tiny microscopic spiral ladder can the truth be found.

In Revelation 21:27 we are told, "*And there shall in no wise enter into it any thing that defileth, neither whatsoever worketh abomination, or maketh a lie: but they which are written in the **Lamb's book of life**.*" This verse says that the book of life belongs to the Lamb, which is Christ, and when we look at the DNA closely we can see evidence for what this verse says.

As you can see from the graphic, our DNA looks like fish from a certain angle, and in the early years of Christianity the fish symbol was used as a symbol for Christ and for Christians. It is perhaps ironic that the Lamb's book of life has the symbol for the Lamb, and it seems as if God has put Christ's name on our DNA. When I look upon the date that the DNA was discovered, I also see an interesting anagram within that date. The number 153 can be found in the numbers, as well as the number 9, which is the sum of 153. So, now we have the fish symbol and the number of fish that was caught into the net.

1953 or 153=9

We are told that only one man was able to open the book of life, and even though it does not state his name in Rev. 5:5, it identifies him by his ancestral roots. In Revelation 5:5 it says, *"And one of the elders saith unto me, Weep not: behold, the Lion of the tribe of Judah, the Root of David, hath prevailed to open the book, and to loose the seven seals thereof."* Jesus Christ came from the tribe of Judah and was a descendant of King David and his nickname of the Lamb was used in other verses to show that he had possession of the book of life.

In Numbers 21, there is a mysterious story that tells of fiery serpents biting the people, and so Moses prayed, and the Lord instructed him to make a fiery serpent and put it on a pole. If we look upon the image that is being conveyed to us with a serpent coiled around a pole, then we can very easily see the spiral helix of a DNA strand.

Illustrators of the 1728 *Figures de la Bible*, Gerard Hoet (1648-1733), and others, published by P. de Hondt in The Hague in 1728

Numbers 21

8 And the LORD said unto Moses, Make thee a fiery serpent, and set it upon a pole: and it shall come to pass, that every one that is bitten, when he looketh upon it, shall live.

9 And Moses made a serpent of brass, and put it upon a pole, and it came to pass, that if a serpent had bitten any man, when he beheld the serpent of brass, he lived.

The image of DNA is clearly being shown to us for the first time, and yet the ancients would not have been able to understand the imagery that they were being shown in these verses. It is only meant to be conveyed to people of our time that have labored to open up the book of life and to see the secrets that it conveys. We can now see that the scientific level of this story is showing us a hidden story within this story, but only for those that endeavor to uncover its secrets from a scientific point of view.

This story is linked with another verse in the Gospels that can add more details to help us figure out what is going on. In John 3:14 Jesus says *"And as Moses lifted up the serpent in the wilderness, even so must the Son of man be lifted up."* Jesus is comparing himself to the serpent that was lifted up on the pole, and remember only one man was able to open the book of life and his name was the Lamb. But what does all these verses really mean, and how can one serpent be used to hurt and kill the Israelites and yet another serpent is being used to heal them? Let's look more closely at this story, and I will show you yet another connection of some earlier verses to show you what is really going on here.

Numbers 21

6 And the LORD sent fiery serpents among the people, and they bit the people; and much people of Israel died.

7 Therefore the people came to Moses, and said, We have sinned, for we have spoken against the LORD, and against thee; pray unto the LORD, that he take away the serpents from us. And Moses prayed for the people.

In Genesis 3 we are told that the serpent tempted Eve to eat of the forbidden fruit, and she did, and as a result she had fallen in her vibratory rate, which led to her becoming physical, and Adam also did the same and became physical as well. In this story, the underlying science is hidden in a homophone. Everything in the physical world is made up of atoms, so once they fell and became physical, they became atoms. A parallel can be made between Adam and atom. Eve's name conveys the darkness that physical objects or people can bring, because Eve is short for evening. In the evening it becomes dark in the night, and all physical objects cast shadows of darkness. In Genesis 1:27 it says "*So God created man in his own image, in the image of God created he him; male and female created he them.*" There was no name given for the male or the female, and it says they were made in God's image. God is spirit as many scriptures describe him/her, and a spirit is not physical. After the fall of mankind, the male and female could be seen in a form. This is when they got their name of Adam and Eve to reflect their physical nature. When light shines on a spiritual being it consumes them as light continues to pass through the being, but when light shines on a physical being, it stops and can not go through them, and as a result a shadow is created behind the being to show an absence of light. The physical being is made of the atom, and they create the darkness of the eve. In Genesis 2, we learn that a change is being made to the image of man, and this one includes dust from the Earth. In Genesis 2:7 it says," *And the LORD God formed man of the dust of the ground, and breathed into his nostrils the breath of life; and man became a living soul.*" It's interesting to note that an experiment done by Gregor Morfill of the Max Planck Institute for Extraterrestrial Physics in Garching, Germany shows that electrically charged dust can organize itself into DNA-like double helixes. Morfill says, "Like DNA, the dust spirals can store information". These experiments that Morfill has done are confirming that dust can make the book of life, which can lead to a human life. Did the Lord open the book of life?

In the second creation, man is no longer made in God's image, because he has become physical, and this is actually when Adam was given his name by the Lord God, and Adam named his wife Eve. The Lord God made Adam and Eve while God was resting on the seventh day. In Genesis 1 the male and female spirits are created by God, and in Genesis 2 the physical man and woman are created by the Lord God. Mankind has a spiritual body and a physical body, but only the physical body blocks the light. We can certainly see the yin/yang in these stories. Our spiritual body is made of light, and our physical body is made of darkness. The light is masculine and the darkness is feminine, so we can see our spiritual and physical body has become together as one body of light and dark, good and evil or yin and yang.

In Genesis 3, we are told that the serpent leads to the fall of mankind, and in Numbers 21 we are told that the fiery serpents are biting the people, and they asked the Lord to be healed from the serpent bites. We can clearly see a big connection between Genesis 3 and Numbers 21 at this point. Here is the key to explaining the connection between the fiery serpents and the DNA. Notice that in Morfill's experiment that the dust has to be electrically charged in order to form the DNA spirals. The name fiery serpents are the key to understanding how the DNA was formed. Electrical charges are seen as fiery sparks of light, and in fact when we look at lightning in the sky, it is not hard to see the connection between a fiery serpent and lightning. Lightning zips back and forth like a snake coils back and forth in its movement, so we can very easily see a comparison being made between the serpent, fiery serpents and lightning in the sky.

Notice in the pattern of lightning we can see branching going on with the fiery serpent as it turns it into fiery serpents. It almost looks like the branching of a tree and if we were to turn it upside down, than we could perhaps see an image of the tree of the knowledge of good and evil within this pattern.

A few years ago I did research on the Seraphim angels and was surprised to learn that Seraph in Hebrew means fiery serpents or flying serpent. This means that the Saraphim angels are associated with the story in Numbers 21, and so we can see that the fiery serpents that the Lord sent among the Israelites are none other than the Seraphim angels. Even though the scriptures say that the Lord sent the Seraphim angels among the people, it does not say that he made them bite the people. We can tell from the scriptures that these serpents were venomous or poisonous to the Israelite people, because it made them die. Likewise, the serpent that tempted Eve to biting the fruit from the tree of knowledge of good and evil also brought an eventual death to Adam and Eve, because all physical life forms do experience death. We are told in Genesis 6:4 that *"There were giants in the earth in those days; and also after that, when the sons of God came in unto the daughters of men, and they bare children to them, the same became mighty men which were of old, men of renown"*. Many Bible scholars interpret this verse to mean the fallen angels had sex with women to produce a hybrid race of giants. In Numbers 21, we are being given the identity of these angels as being from the Seraphim order of the Heavenly Angels. The Seraphim angels were the ones that were biting the Israelites, but they were biting them in a symbolic way. The sexual organs of a male looks much like a serpent, only these Seraphim were leaving behind a sperm that was genetically contaminating the Israelites, so therefore the fiery serpents were poisoning the people.

In Numbers 21, we can see that there were two different Seraphim angels, because some fiery serpents were biting the people and another fiery serpent was healing the people. The fiery serpent on the pole was Jesus Christ, as he says in John 3:14, so we can see that Jesus Christ must represent a DNA change of some sort, because his DNA was meant to heal the Israelite people of the serpent bites. This is how Jesus Christ was the only man that could open this book that was talked about in Revelation 5:5, because the prophecies in Numbers 21 shows that his DNA is one that will heal the mixed genetics of the Israelite people, thus correcting the genetic breach that occurred in Genesis 6. Furthermore, in Genesis 49:11 the prophecy of Jesus says that he is the choice vine and that he will be banded to the vineyard of the Israelites. In Genesis 49:11 it says, **"Binding his foal unto the vine**, *and his ass's colt unto the* **choice vine**; *he washed his garments in wine, and his clothes in the blood of grapes"*. The only way for Jesus to spread the new genetics to correct the problems that occurred between the mixing of the Seraphim angels and the Israelites was for him to spread a new seed in the vineyard by binding or grafting his genetic vine into the vineyard of the Israelites. This plan could only be carried out through reproduction, and so this is further proof that Jesus would have gotten married and had children to perpetuate the genetics of a new bloodline that we call the Grails.

It's interesting that John 3:14 talks about how the fiery serpent on the pole was lifted up and that the Son of man will be lifted up also, which was information that we were not privy to in the Numbers 21 story. The Numbers 21 story simply says that the fiery serpent was set or put upon the pole, but Jesus says it was lifted up. Remember, the chapter on the Solfeggio tones where I said it was interesting that the Israelite people kept pitching after that story before they sang. Jesus words' of being lifted up and the pitching that occurred with the Israelite people suggest that this healing DNA change was meant to lift or raise the vibratory rate of the DNA and the people to prepare them for the harvest or ascension. As I pointed out before, the word pitch can be used as a musical term, but it also can mean to rise or fall, and in the Numbers 21 story, I would suggest it could also mean to rise.

[4]*pitch* noun b (1) : the property of a sound and especially a musical tone that is determined by the frequency of the waves producing it : highness or lowness of sound (2) : a standard frequency for tuning instruments

In Revelation 21, there is a reference to the Lamb's book of life in verse 27. It says that no one can enter into New Jerusalem except those that are written in the Lamb's book of life. It is interesting that this whole chapter is hinting around about the Fibonacci sequence with the measurements for the wall of New Jerusalem being 144 cubits. The number of the chapter is 21, which is also a Fibonacci number. The DNA measures 34 angstroms long by 21 angstroms wide for each full cycle of its double helix spiral. These numbers in Revelation 21 are hinting around about the structure of DNA being in a Phi spiral shape, which is also called the golden spiral.

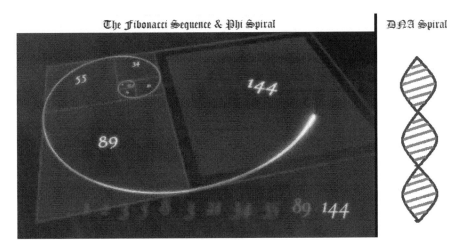

Mark E. Curtis began an investigation 20 years ago into the structure of the DNA and he ended up making a realignment change in the spiral based on geometrical principles. He found that the DNA spiral forms ten regular pentagons orientated about a decagon when it moves in one rotation, and a decagon is a ten sided polygon. What I find most interesting about the DNA spiral tracing out a decagon for every full revolution is that the degrees of the inside angles of a decagon is 144 degrees. Perhaps this was another hint in Revelation 21:17 to the spiral motion of the DNA double helix.

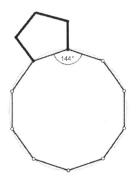

Another interesting connection that I have found between the decagon pattern of DNA and the Solfeggio tones is that a skip rate number comes up in the measure of exterior angles of a regular decagon. If you measure all of the outside angles on a decagon, it would be 36 degrees for each one, so you would multiply it by the number of vertices to get the 360 degrees of a circle. (i.e. 36 º X 10= 360 º) The exterior angle of a polygon is 360 degrees minus the interior angle, so for the regular decagon we must subtract 36 degrees from 360 degrees to find the answer of 324 degrees.

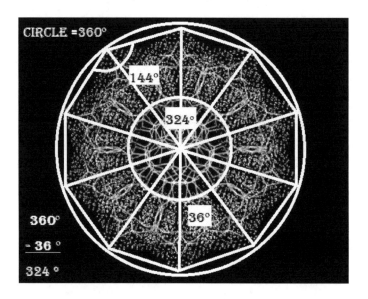

The number 324 is in the skip rate of the Solfeggio tone math and is a multiple of 108. The interior angles of a pentagon are 108 degrees. There are many interesting connections between the Solfeggio tones and the DNA.

111 111 ⟨21⟩ 111 111 102 111 111 Skip rate numbers
/3 /3 /3 /3 /3   /3 /3 /3
37 37   7 37 37 ⟨34⟩37 37   Prime Numbers
                    ▼
                 (Even #)

DNA is 34 angstroms long and 21 angstroms wide.

243   324   432   Triplet skip rate numbers
/3   /3   /3
81   108   144

The numbers 81 and 108 are skip rate numbers between skip rates 21, 102 & 210. The number 144 is in Revelation 21 and is the interior angle of a decagon, which is the pattern of DNA.

The interior angles on a pentagon are 108 degrees, and the DNA traces out ten regular pentagons orientated about a decagon for each revolution.

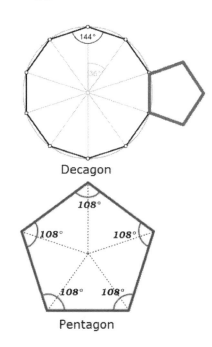

Decagon

Pentagon

84

Dr. Robert Langridge made an image of what the DNA would look like if we could make it stand up on one end and look down at it from the top view of the DNA. It shows an image that has 10 vertices, and this image confirms that it is in the shape of a decagon.

**View Along the Axis
of the β DNA Double Helix**

Picture By: Dr. Robert Langridge

In Revelation 21, we are being shown the shape of the DNA as it presently exists, but we also seem to be shown that our DNA will be changing into a new shape. The DNA has 10 vertices now, but it could perhaps mutate into 12 vertices. In 1 Corinthians 15:52 we are told *"In a moment, in the twinkling of an eye, at the last trump: for the trumpet shall sound, and the dead shall be raised incorruptible, and **we shall be changed**"*. Revelation 21 seems to be telling us what our present day DNA looks like, but at the same time it is also confirming what we will become on the new Earth when we change in the twinkling of an eye.

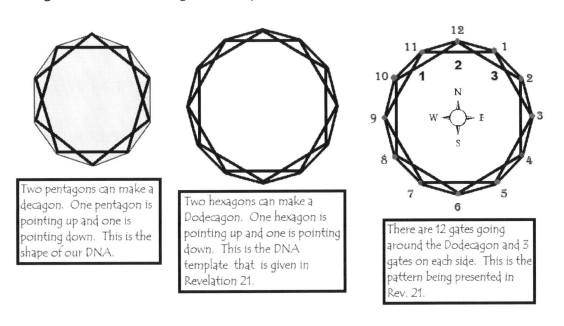

Two pentagons can make a decagon. One pentagon is pointing up and one is pointing down. This is the shape of our DNA.

Two hexagons can make a Dodecagon. One hexagon is pointing up and one is pointing down. This is the DNA template that is given in Revelation 21.

There are 12 gates going around the Dodecagon and 3 gates on each side. This is the pattern being presented in Rev. 21.

85

In the many chapters of this book, we have been seeing the same image over and over of the hexagon pattern, so it seems quite ironic that the pattern for New Jerusalem seems to be two hexagons making a twelve sided dodecagon. Our present day DNA traces out a decagon made with 10 pentagons, so it seems obvious that the next step in our DNA change would be to form a dodecagon with 12 hexagons. This is the pattern that we have been presented with over and over in the Bible as being the Spirit of God, and Jesus came to bring us the Holy Spirit. In Revelation 21, we are shown the DNA pattern of the tree of knowledge of good and evil and the pattern for the tree of life.

Remember the Holy of Holies cube can be traced out inside of a hexagon, so with the New Jerusalem pattern, we have two cubes. This is showing the pattern of a cube from a fourth dimensional point of view. The cube becomes a hypercube in the fourth dimension, and a hypercube's shadow would form a cube within a cube. This encoded information is showing us hyperdimensional geometry, which is also telling us that the new Earth is in a higher dimension. The DNA looks like a spiral staircase, and it makes me think of Jacob's ladder to Heaven. We can see from the blueprint patterns that are encoded in Revelation 21 that our DNA has to be lifted up or raised in frequency to be able to cross over into a higher dimension. Therefore, we can look at Jacob's ladder as being more like the keys of a piano spiraling up like a DNA ladder and to open up the door into the next dimension, we must have the higher vibration of the new song of Christ, and we must have the Lamb's book of life.

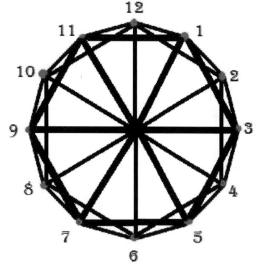

TWO CUBES OF NEW JERUSALEM

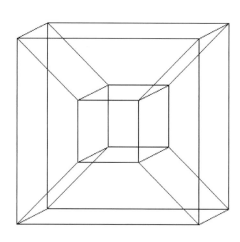

HYPERCUBE & TESSERACT

There is symbolism of the DNA in the imagery of the serpent coiled around the tree of knowledge of good and evil, as the DNA is also coiled in a spiral manner like a snake is spiraled around a tree. It is also interesting to note that ever since the fall of mankind, another tree has sprouted up that did not exist before, and that is the family tree. The first book of the Bible is called Genesis, and within that word is a clue to the nature of the family tree. A gene is a hereditary unit that is transferred from a parent to their offspring, and it determines some of the characteristics of the offspring. Half of the DNA from the father and the mother is what is inherited by every human being, as we grow this family tree branch by branch from the roots of Adam and Eve. This tree could only grow from our DNA splitting and mingling with someone else's DNA to create new life. In Jeremy Narby's book "The Cosmic Serpent: DNA and the Origins of Knowledge", he points out that every culture from around the world has serpent symbols much like our Bible does in the book of Genesis and Numbers. He believes that this ancient symbolism of the serpent is referring to the DNA of mankind, and I would agree with his perspective. The image of a serpent coiled around a tree or pole is eerily similar to the DNA helix that is coiled throughout our body. Eating the fruit that the serpent offered Eve has actually made serpents all throughout our body, and so we perhaps became infected by that fruit, as the old saying goes "you are what you eat".

The Staff of Hermes   The Rod of Asclepius

The modern day medical symbol for healing is the caduceus and as you can see in the image on the left it looks just like the spiral double helix of the DNA.

The Old Testament traces the genealogy of the Israelite people from Adam and Eve to the time of Jesus. This family tree grew from just two genetic seeds in the beginning. The New Testament traces the genealogy from Jesus Christ to our present time. Perhaps the net that is talked about in John 21 could be a ge**net**ic net that has spread since the grail bloodline has begun. If this genetic net vibrates higher and higher in pitch, then perhaps the serpent will be raised on the pole as Jesus talked about in John 3:14. In Numbers 21 the Israelites had a brass serpent on the pole, and they kept pitching after that until they finally sang their song, so perhaps the 144,000 from the tribes of Israel will finally be able to sing the new song, and that song will be of a higher frequency to help raise the fish in the net. It's interesting that the tribe of Dan is not mentioned with the 12 tribes of Israel in Revelation 7. We can find more symbolism to suggest that perhaps the new song has something to do with our DNA changing to higher frequencies, because the tribe of Dan being left out shows us a clue. One anagram from the name DAN is DNA, but the symbolism even goes further than this clue. In Genesis 49:17 we are told "*Dan* (DNA) *shall be a **serpent** by the way, an adder in the path, that biteth the horse heels, so that his rider shall fall backward*". We are being told that the serpent is the DNA in chapter 17, and the number 17 is a divisor for the number 153, so this suggest that the DNA serpent will be raised up in Jesus Christ's genetic net.

We all carry within our bodies the book of life and within that book is our entire life story: our joy, our pain, our love, our temptations, our strengths, our weaknesses, our successes, our failures and everything that makes us who we are. It's perhaps a blessing that geneticists don't know how to read 97% of its contents, because within this book is all of our secrets. The Bible tells us that we will be judged out of this book, not by man, but by God. We could indeed think of this place as being like a school, and the DNA book of life would contain our homework, our schoolwork and our report card. Some tests we passed, and some tests we failed, but all of the results of every test that we have faced are kept inside of this tiny microscopic book. It is perhaps a sobering thought to know that "*every idle word that men shall speak, they shall give account thereof in the day of judgment*" as it says in Matthew 12:36. Knowing that our DNA is recording everything that we do or say lets us know that at every second, minute or hour of the day...God is watching us. Though we keep secrets from one another, there are no secrets to God, so we have to ask ourselves: "Am I here to impress man or God?" Well, the answer lies within each and every one of us like a serpent coiled around the tree of knowledge of good and evil, but hopefully some day soon through our actions, we will be able to transform that tree into the tree of life.

Revelation 2:7 *He that hath an ear, let him hear what the Spirit saith unto the churches; To him that overcometh will I give to eat of the tree of life, which is in the midst of the paradise of God.*

PHYSICS

John 14:2 In my Father's house are many mansions: if it were not so, I would have told you. I go to prepare a place for you.

Many people are not even aware that there are a lot of physics encoded into the Bible. In John 14:2, Jesus talks about how there are many mansions in his Father's house. We can take this to mean two different things, but only one explanation makes the most sense to me. The first interpretation could be that there are many planets in the universe, but if this were to be the case then Jesus would have left in a spaceship and then returned a few years later to take us back to the planet he prepared for us. The second interpretation is that Jesus was talking about there being many different dimensions in the universe, and this one makes more sense considering the fact that he died, was resurrected and then ascended into Heaven. The physicists say that the mathematical equations used in string theory have proven that other spatial dimensions are possible. In M-theory there is even a possibility that perhaps 11 dimensions exist altogether. I have already shown you that Revelation 21's blueprint for New Jerusalem implies a hypercube with the two cubes in the dodecagon, so hyperdimensional geometry is being presented to us.

The Bible also encodes other examples of dimensions in the Tabernacle pattern. The veil or curtain going in between the Tabernacle and the Holy of Holies is an example of a membrane that goes in between two dimensions. The only way to get through a membrane is through a wormhole, which is also known as an Einstein Rosen bridge. This theory states that there are rips or tears within the fabric of space-time, which causes tunnels to form. Wormholes can happen within this universe to connect one area to another, but they also can go through a membrane into a higher or lower dimension of space. The name Holy of Holies is a homophone, and the first word Holy sounds exactly like the word holey. The word holy means that something or someone is dedicated or consecrated to God or a religious purpose, and it also means sacred. The word holey means to have holes and if you take out the "I" in holies you would have holes. The name of the Holy of Holies is meant to be a clue to the wormhole. The Holy of Holies in the Tabernacle and the Temple was in a cube shape, and in Revelation 21 the template shows a hypercube, so therefore we are being shown the way to get into a higher dimension is through a wormhole.

There are still other interesting examples of wormholes in the Bible, and the main example is the stories that involve whirlwinds. A whirlwind is defined as being a column of air that moves rapidly in a cylindrical or funnel shape. We are told that Elijah ascended to somewhere else in a whirlwind in the book of Kings. In 2 Kings 2:1 it says *"And it came to pass, when the Lord would **take up Elijah into heaven by a whirlwind**, that Elijah went with Elisha from Gilgal"*. The word gilgal in Hebrew actually means a wheel, rolling thing or a whirlwind, so we are seeing in this verse that the village of Gilgal is actually a name describing the event that happened there. There actually is a stone circle located at the ancient town of Gilgal, and it looks similar to other stone circles in other parts of the world.

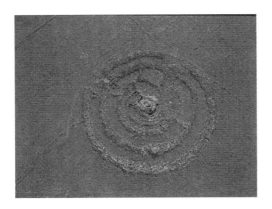

A wormhole is similar to a black hole, and it swirls around in a spiral motion. The spiral motion is confirmed by the Fibonacci sequence that was encoded in Revelation 21, and as I talked about in another chapter the Fibonacci numbers form the spacing in a Phi spiral. If we ever saw a wormhole, we would definitely compare it to a whirlwind, although it would not be destructive like a black hole or tornado. In the Elijah story we are being shown some examples of wormholes throughout the story. In 2 Kings 2:8 it says *"And Elijah took his mantle, and wrapped it together, and smote the waters, and they were divided hither and thither, so that they two went over on dry ground"*. This mysterious verse is telling us that Elijah put on his cloak, and then he strikes the waters to make them divide, which is similar to the story of Moses making the Red Sea divide with his rod. It's interesting because if we read this verse from an allegorical viewpoint, it is the same thing that Physicists say about a wormhole, because a wormhole is caused when the fabric of space-time is ripped or divided to create a tunnel. This story is also mysterious because it seems as if Elijah needs the cloak in order to perform this miraculous feat: like Moses needed the rod to part the sea.

When Jesus died, there was a rip in the veil of the temple, so we are being told that a wormhole was opened up for his soul to ascend through, and so Jesus Christ went through the Holy of Holies. Upon opening up this doorway, the scriptures also say that many saints also were lifted out of their graves, and they would have ascended through a wormhole as well. In Matthew 27:51 it says, *"And, behold, the veil of the temple was rent in twain from the top to the bottom; and the earth did quake, and the rocks rent."*

We must remember that the veil that was rent was not in the physical Temple, but was in his temple body, as in John 21 it says that Jesus "*spake of the temple of his body*". It is ironic that people that have near death experiences talk about how a tunnel just opens up out of nowhere upon their death. It seems more than a coincidence that physicists explain wormholes as ripping open the fabric of space-time, and that the veil in the temple was ripped upon Jesus death. The veil that was rent in the physical Temple is an analogy of the rip that occurs in Jesus' temple body after his death. In Matthew 27:52 it says, "*And the graves were opened; and many bodies of the saints which slept arose*". The resurrection that was prophesied happened and the saints arose through the wormhole, so it is interesting that verse 51 talks about the veil being rent, and we know that 51 is a multiple of the John 21 number of 153. So, we can actually see that Jesus net was now deployed into the Cosmic Sea of the third dimension, and that now others were journeying through the ripped veil of space-time. The wormhole models of physicists often show it looking like a net, and so we can see the fish were being gathered in Jesus net of the harvest. His third time that he was seen after his death was when he helped the Apostles to catch 153 fish, and so now he is encouraging his followers to help him to fish for more souls of men. The near death experience confirms that the net is working perfectly to help souls ascend to the other side.

The Solfeggio tone numbers of 3, 6 and 9 are also encoded into the story of Jesus death and ascension. It says in Matthew 27:45, "*Now from the **sixth** hour there was darkness over all the land unto the **ninth** hour*". Jesus body remained in the tomb for 3 days, so we can see that the numbers of the Solfeggio tones are encoded in this chapter, and that this is also implying a connection with Jesus fishing net.

In 2 Kings 2:11 it says "*And it came to pass, as they still went on, and talked, that, behold, there appeared a chariot of fire, and horses of fire, and parted them both asunder; and Elijah went up by a whirlwind into heaven*". This verse shows the actual formation of the wormhole and some kind of object within the wormhole that looks like fire. In Michio Kaku's book "Beyond Einstein", he describes what it would be like to encounter higher dimensional beings or objects. He says, "We would see objects appear, change color, grow and shrink in size, and then suddenly disappear". Apparently, we would only be seeing a three dimensional cross section of the higher dimensional object, because we are in a lower dimension. It would be hard to even make sense of what we were seeing, because our perceptions would only be limited to one, two and three dimensional objects. The scriptures talk about him seeing a chariot of fire and horses of fire, but the observers were only looking at the object from a three dimensional perspective, so they were trying to describe it with objects that they know.

Fire is ever changing and dynamic in its movement, and fire displays a variety of colors from yellow, orange, blue and violet, so we can definitely see that Dr. Kaku's description of what a higher dimensional object would look like seems to apply to what Elijah and Elisha saw inside the wormhole or whirlwind.

A cartoon flip book demonstrates hyperdimensional space quite simply. If you flip each page at a constant rate, then you get to see a neat animated clip or movie; however, if you flip the pages too fast, you will only see a blur or invisible pages. We could think of the motion created by flipping the pages, as being the vibratory rate of a human being and the dimensions by which the being encounters. If we don't flip the first page, then we are focusing on a two dimensional object, and therefore we are stuck in a two dimensional reality. Now how do we get unstuck from this reality? Well, we must start flipping the pages quickly, and then we find that we are encountering something that we have not been exposed to before. We start to see the concept of motion, time and the new dimension of height. This isn't just one two dimensional page, but we find that there are other pages behind the first one and so height gets added to our page, and it becomes an actual book. We can experience this for awhile and focus on this steady rate of vibration in flipping the pages at a constant speed. We get to see things like motion and time in this three dimensional book, and all of these concepts are quite real in our universe. Again though, we can start to get stuck in this reality until that is all that we are focusing on, and we can't see any more realities than this one. We can switch back and forth between the second dimension and the third dimension, but we can't quite see into a higher dimension yet. Death would kind of be like coming to the end of the book, and being unable to flip anymore pages. Without flipping the pages, there is no more time or motion, so you might want to go back to the first page and try to flip again even faster to see if there might be something that you missed in this book of life. Now, you could start to flip the pages really fast and at a higher vibration of speed, and what you find out is that everything disappears, as if by some magic trick. This would be the fourth dimension, and in this one you can't even measure motion or linear time, so this would be like the end of time. Linear time is only a reality in the third dimension, but as we break away from this dimension and go into the next one, linear time will not exist. If you can't see the motion of an object, then you can't measure time. In fact, a nice trick of going into the fourth dimension would be that everyone has become a prophet, because even though you are no longer experiencing time, you would still be able to see the timeline as a whole. You would be above the linear plane of time, and thus you would become an observer to time and able to see everything that has ever happened within the three dimensional space-time continuum. Another trick of going from the third dimension to the fourth dimension is that you would effectively leave the darkness behind, because the illusion of the darkness is caused by the blocking of light from a physical object. The fourth dimension would absolutely be a dimension of light. If you could flip the pages very fast in this book, then the actual book would disappear and all you would see would be the light flowing through the book.

It is somewhat ironic that the Bible describes our DNA as being the book of life. The book of life is like a spiral stairway to Heaven, except at each dimensional level perhaps we must increase our vibratory rate to get through the door to the next level.

There are other encounters with wormholes in the Bible, such as Ezekiel seeing an object come out of a whirlwind in the north and the Lord talking to Job out of a whirlwind. These stories make no sense if people believe that the Bible is talking about a tornado, but substitute the modern day name of wormhole instead of a whirlwind and the stories make perfect sense. If you have seen the movie Stargate or the Stargate shows on television, then you start to get an idea of what these stories are really talking about with the whirlwind encounters. The Bible has always been thought of as being a mystical or magical book filled with miracles, paranormal encounters, Angel encounters and prophecy, but when we start to view these stories from a level of science and math, then the stories become something like science fiction. Everything that happens in the Bible has a logical explanation from a modern day point of view, because with applied scientific explanations the whirlwinds become wormholes and the many mansions that Jesus talked about become dimensions. As Arthur C. Clarke once said "Any sufficiently advanced technology is indistinguishable from magic".

If I was to go visit an isolated tribe in the jungles of South America and bring them up here to America in an airplane, then as they would encounter each kind of technology, they would assume that I have great magical powers. It's not that magic doesn't exist, but it's just that our magic is done in a scientific way. Just because the Bible was written in ancient times does not mean that magic or miracles were done without science. To truly understand the paranormal events that happened in the Bible, we must take a scientific perspective. If a fourth dimensional being were to come through a wormhole right now and tell us all of the events that were about to occur, we may believe it to be a mystical or a magical encounter, because we haven't yet encountered a higher dimension. The movie Mothman shows this concept of a higher dimensional being trying to warn mankind of an impending disaster. What is a futuristic event to us would not be one to a higher dimensional being, so it would be a possibility to warn three dimensional beings. This is what we have in the prophecies of the Bible, only the prophecies in the Bible are not trying to prevent a catastrophe, but they seemed to be used to help prepare us.

From a scientific point of view, we know that a fourth dimensional being would be able to see our entire timeline as a whole; therefore it would not be a miracle to them, but just a reality we have yet to know. Here is an example from the two dimensional world of Flatland. If you or I were to take a wormhole ride down to the second dimension to see what it is like there, we would actually find out that we will have super powers that would astound the flatlanders. There is one example that was shown in the documentary "What the bleep do we know?" in an animated short about Flatland. A superhero goes through a wormhole into the second dimension, and he starts talking to a circle in a rectangle house. She believes the being to be a ghost or either God, because she can't really see him in a form she understands. All she would see would be a weird 2-D version of the 3-D man, because she doesn't yet know about height, nor can she see it or experience that reality. Many people in our third dimension also have encounters with beings from a higher dimension, but most are regarded as being crazy when they talk about their encounter. Okay, to get back to our story, the circle demands to have some proof that this voice is coming from a higher dimension. The man starts to name everything that is in a closed room in the house. The circle is astounded and thinks that this is completely impossible, but the proof shows his words to be the truth.

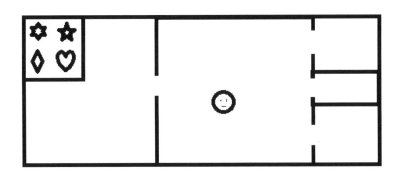

Can you name what is in the locked room?

Here is your chance to be a superhero with special powers. How easy is it to name everything that is inside the locked room in the house in Flatland? It's pretty simple, right? There is a Star of David, a five pointed star or pentagram, a diamond and a heart. We can see everything in the locked room because we have the advantage of having height, so we can see over the two dimensional lines. Remember though, that the circle in this house doesn't have height, so they can't see past the lines. Closed line areas would be barriers to 2-D lifeforms, but not to us. A barrier to us would be that a house has walls and a roof, and we would not be able to see what is kept inside of a locked room, unless of course we could manage to find a key to open the room. Now imagine if we were inside of our house when a higher dimensional being visits us, and they start to tell us what is inside of a locked safe we have in our closet. It would totally astound us and perplex us as we would not be able to understand how this being could know such a thing. A higher dimensional being is going to have an advantage on us because they will be able to see, experience and know things that we do not know. To a higher dimensional being walls are not barriers and neither are roofs or locked safes. A fourth dimensional being would absolutely be a prophet and they would be able to tell us all kinds of events that have not happened yet, and of course, a time traveler would be able to do this as well. You might say that this is not possible, but physicists are telling us that their mathematical formulas are showing them that other dimensions do exist beyond this one. If the math is showing this to be the case, than there must be something to these formulas, because math does not lie.

This kind of gives a whole new perspective to the prophecies in the Bible, because the explanation of a fourth dimension would definitely explain the knowing of future events. If I was to encounter a 4th dimensional being that tells me all kinds of events that will happen in the future, and I write them down for the world, then would it not be the same as the prophets that wrote the predictions in the Bible? Prophecies don't make logical sense from our dimensional perspective, but from a higher dimensional point of view, everything can be explained with physics.

Imagine a boat on the surface of the sea and a fisherman getting ready to cast his net into the water. This fisherman lives on the surface, but there is a whole new world underneath him below. He can interact with that world temporarily by swimming in the ocean or scuba diving below with an air tank, but he can't live there permanently. Now up above the fisherman is the sky and then outer space is just beyond that level. He can temporarily fly in planes, but he can't live there. He might have an opportunity if he is lucky to go into space, as well, but he would only be able to live there for short periods of time and not permanently. We can see that even from our three dimensional perspective there are worlds within worlds here that are hidden from our view. If we went down even further, there is a microscopic world that we can see with telescopes and know that it exists, but we can't communicate with its lifeforms, nor can we live there. Now imagine all of the dimensions are surrounding us, we can't see them or experience them yet, but we know that they are there. Now imagine that God, our Creator is in the highest dimension of all and in that dimension he can see all other dimensions. God would know everything that ever was, is and will be. This was who inspired our Bible, and nothing would be impossible to God in this higher dimension. God would be able to interact in all dimensions, whereas we can only interact in three dimensions. This is the majesty and awe of God's kingdom, and even though we can not experience it all just yet, the Bible is giving us clues to what all exists beyond our world.

Another example of wormholes in the Bible is the bells that were used on the high priest garments. In Exodus 28:33 it says *"And beneath upon the hem of it thou shalt make pomegranates of blue, and of purple, and of scarlet, round about the hem thereof; and **bells** of gold between them round about"*. The mouth to a wormhole looks very much like the shape of a bell. Bells also make sounds or tones, so this is another clue. The pomegranates colors are also reflecting the Phi colors that 70% of the Solfeggio tones display. As I wrote in a previous chapter the number 144 in Revelation 21 is a Fibonacci number and the Fibonacci sequence of numbers displays the Phi spiral, which is also known as the golden spiral. This is another hint as to what the Holy of Holies looks like, because a wormhole spirals at the entrance or mouth which leads into the throat or tunnel.

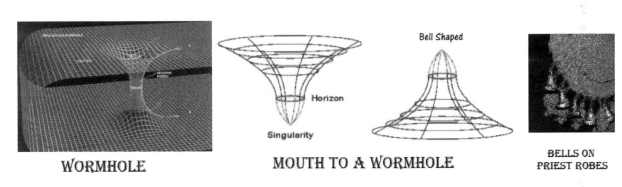

WORMHOLE MOUTH TO A WORMHOLE BELLS ON PRIEST ROBES

There is a physics clue in our Bible that tells us about all the energy in our universe, but if read strictly from a literal point of view, it is only talking about a lamp. In Numbers 8 it says, *"Speak unto Aaron and say unto him, When thou lightest the lamps, the seven lamps shall give light over against the candlestick"*. We have to ask ourselves about what is so important about having a 7 candlestick lamp to be made in the Tabernacle? Of course, the obvious answer it that it gives light on the inside of the building so people can see. Most people would think that the number of seven is to commemorate the Creation of the world in seven days, but remember the heavens and the earth were made in six days and the seventh day was a day of rest. There is another clue that might help us to resolve what this pattern could be talking about in the Menorah. In Revelation 4:5 the verse says *"And out of the throne proceeded lightnings and thunderings and voices: and there were **seven lamps of fire** burning before the throne, which are the **seven Spirits of God**"*. The seven lamps of fire is the Menorah and notice how it is being compared to the seven spirits of God. There are seven forms of electromagnetic energy in our universe and astronomers have viewed the universe in many of those different forms to help them to understand how our universe works.

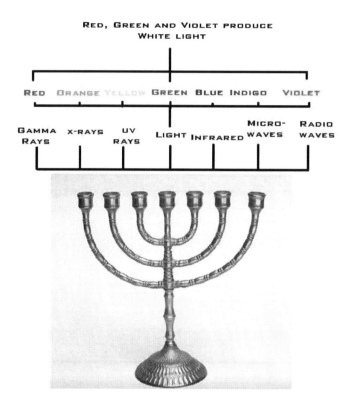

The seven forms of the electromagnetic scale are gamma rays, X-rays, ultraviolet rays, visible light, infrared waves, microwaves and radio waves. These are the seven spirits of God that the seven candlestick lamp of the Menorah is symbolically showing us if we read these verses from a scientific point of view. Notice that light is at the center of the electromagnetic scale, and this is symbolically showing us that Christ is at the center of the scale because Christ said that he was the light. Jesus says in John 9:5, "*As long as I am in the world, **I am the light** of the world*". You can think of the EM scale as being like a weighing scale and the light is at the center and perfectly balanced.

The Menorah also represents many other symbolic interpretations, as well. In Genesis 9:16 we are told, "*And the bow shall be in the cloud; and I will look upon it, that I may remember the everlasting covenant between God and every living creature of all flesh that is upon the earth*". This rainbow that God gave to mankind shows the seven primary colors of red, orange, yellow, green, blue, indigo and violet. The Solfeggio tones are also found within the colors of the visible light area of the electromagnetic scale. The color scale is like a Menorah within the Menorah, because it would be a seven color scale within the middle of the electromagnetic scale.

98

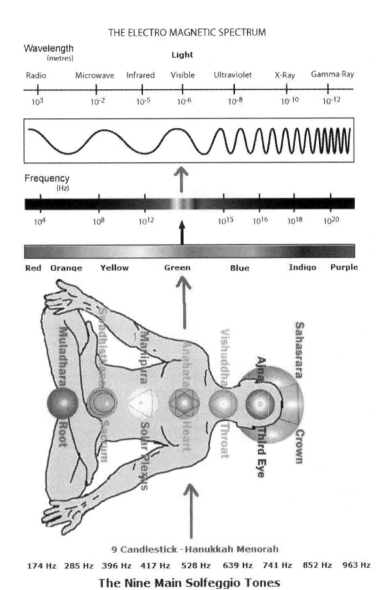

THE ELECTRO MAGNETIC SPECTRUM

9 Candlestick - Hanukkah Menorah

174 Hz   285 Hz   396 Hz   417 Hz   528 Hz   639 Hz   741 Hz   852 Hz   963 Hz

The Nine Main Solfeggio Tones
528Hz--greenish-yellow

The chakra scale is another scale that could be presented symbolically in the Menorah pattern, although this may seem a controversial topic to most Christians. The chakras are considered energy centers in the body, but from another point of view they are the 7 main endocrine glands. On the graphic of the EM scale, 7 primary colors, 7 chakras and the Solfeggio tones, it shows that light, the green color, the heart and the middle tone of the 9 Solfeggio scale all matches up in the center. This shows the perfect balance of the three seven scales lined up together. The 7 primary colors are often matched with the 7 chakras and the heart chakra is the color green. In John 2:21 it says that Jesus "*spake of the temple of his body*", and so we can easily see that the 7 chakras or energy centers would fit the template of the 7 candlestick Menorah for the temple body.

On the chapter about astronomy I revealed that Taurus was the first precession constellation in the Tabernacle star map. Another interesting hint that the Holy of Holies in the Tabernacle is referring to a wormhole kind of holey can be found with the pronunciation of Taurus. First, let me explain that a wormhole is in the middle of a torus like pattern of energy. A torus looks like a donut with a hole in the middle, so it is quite ironic that a homophone for torus is Taurus. These two words are pronounced the exact same way, so the Bible is giving us another interesting clue to the wormhole in the name of the Taurus constellation.

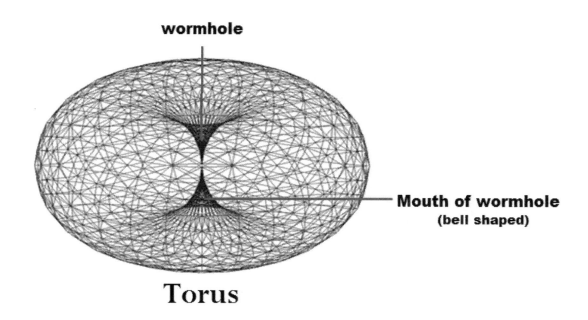

wormhole

Mouth of wormhole
(bell shaped)

Torus

Stan Tenan of the Meru Foundation discovered that there is a lot of geometry being encoded in the Hebrew letters. He took the first verse in the Bible and counted the Hebrew letters in base-3, and then they paired up. He then put each letter on a bead and chain and curled it around until the same letters matched up. He made a beautiful torus pattern with the Hebrew letters of Genesis 1:1. In Genesis 1:1 the Bible says, "*In the beginning God created the heaven and the earth*", and the underlying geometry shows that it was created with the toroidal energy form. Some scientists have suggested that our entire universe may be shaped like a torus, and the toroidal energy pattern is being used as a way to come up with free energy devices called zero point energy. The potential for using toroidal energy as a clean source of energy has been promoted in a documentary called Thrive and it can currently be viewed for free on You Tube.

When I first started to realize that there was a lot of physics in the Bible I got really excited at the possibilities of learning to understand this scientific level that had been interwoven into the underlying pattern of the stories and the Tabernacle pattern, as well as the many other various patterns that are displayed over and over again within the Bible. The physics level of the Bible gives a whole new meaning to the Holy Bible, as the universe has turned out to be a very holey place. Astronomers have discovered that our Milky Way galaxy has a black hole at the center, and all of the matter revolving around this hole is spiraling around in much the same way that water forms into whirlpools as it goes down a drain. Elijah took a ride in a whirlwind to Heaven, and the Lord talked to Job through a whirlwind, so it seems mighty interesting that a whirling wormhole could be the Holy of Holies. You may say that there is a hole in this theory or that something mighty fishy is going on here, but I say go fishing for yourself and discover the true net that Jesus Christ is talking about, as it is a very holey net indeed.

ELECTRICITY

Numbers 3:31 And their charge shall be the ark, and the table, and the candlestick, and the altars, and the vessels of the sanctuary wherewith they minister, and the hanging, and all the service thereof.

Many Bible Scholars and scientists now believe that the Ark of the Covenant was some type of an electrical capacitor, and that an electrical charge went in between the two cherubim at the top of the ark. Some of the words of the verses referring to the ark imply that there is an electrical connection, and also it's interesting that the word ark itself could be a homophone for arc. The word arc means a luminous electrical discharge between two electrodes or other points. In Numbers 3:31 it says that the Levite priest charge shall be the ark. These very words are suggestive of an electrical charge that goes together with an electrical arc. Reading this verse from a strictly literal point of view would make it sound like the priest just took care of the ark, but if we read the wording of charge and ark/arc from an electrical perspective, it gets much more interesting. This verse is kind of hinting around at the electricity component of the ark. An electrical charge is positive, negative or neutral within the atom which makes up all known matter. Particles with an electric charge interact with each other through the electromagnetic force to create electric fields, and remember the electromagnetic spectrum is represented in the Bible as the 7 candlestick Menorah and also called the 7 Spirits of God. So to put this in another way, the atoms/Adams are interacting with the Spirit of God to create electricity, and when they are in motion they also create magnetic fields. The electromag**net**ic fields around the Earth are made by this interaction, so in a way this is another explanation of the net of John 21, and in another chapter I will explain that the ley lines on the Earth channel some of this energy.

The Numbers 21 story has DNA and Solfeggio tones interpretations of the brass serpent on the pole, but it can also have an electrical lesson for us to study as well. The Bible's stories were written in such a way that it can compact as much information within a little amount of space, because they could use one parable to convey many different things by using similar connections. In other words, the Bible used the serpent spiraling around a pole to show the structure of a spiraling DNA, sine waves and how to make electricity. Remember the fiery serpents are like the electrical lightning bolts in the sky, and so looking at this story from this perspective, we can see the brass serpent as being like a copper wire wrapped around a pole or tube to produce electricity.

When I was a kid my dad used to show me and my sister how to produce electricity and make a generator. I can remember him wrapping the copper wire around a rod and then using a magnet near the copper wire to produce electricity. I was in awe of how easy it was to make electricity, and I have always remembered my dad teaching us this science lesson.

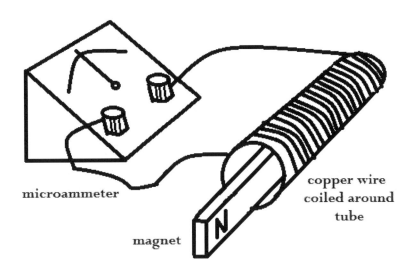

microammeter

magnet

copper wire coiled around tube

The brass serpent going around the pole reminds me of copper wire going around a rod, and brass in biblical times was an alloy of copper and tin. It's easy to see that this story could also be demonstrating how to make the fiery serpent of electricity. The pole that the brass serpent is wrapped around can also have a double meaning, and therefore be talking about the pole of a magnet, simultaneously while talking about the rod. There is a north and south pole on a magnet and they repel each other, whereas like poles attract. There are many representations of magnets having a positive and negative side, which is the same way electricity, works. For an example, a car battery has a positive and negative connector for wires and also has a ground wire.

As I brought up in another chapter, the Numbers 21 story is also talking about the Solfeggio tones, so I find it ironic that the tones are positive, negative and neutral. The tones have the same positive, negative and neutral charges as the particles inside of an atom. In an atom the proton is positive, the electron is negative and the neutron is neutral, so the Bible is showing a pattern that exists from the microscopic world to the macroscopic world. In the electrical world there is a positive wire, a negative wire and a ground wire. Perhaps the ground wire can be thought of as being neutral, since it does not create an electrical charge and is considered to have zero voltage.

The most astounding thing that I have discovered has to do with a mysterious castle in southern Florida that was made by just one man. A man named Ed Leedskalnin moved from Latvia to America and later settled in the south of Florida in 1923 when he became ill with Tuberculosis. Somehow he managed to cure himself despite the fact that his doctor had only given him 6 months to live. He bought some land and began to quarry coral stones and build a castle all by himself. He had no cranes or modern machinery and the stones weighed tons. The heaviest stone actually weighs 30 tons and was used as part of a display that resembles the King's chamber of the Great Pyramid. He used a 9 ton stone for a swivel door or gate, and it was positioned so perfectly balanced that it could be pushed open with a finger. The 9 ton gate broke and had to be repaired in 1986, and even though Ed made it himself, it took a 20 ton crane, crane operator, engineer and a crew of five two weeks to repair the gate. I went there in 2010 and the gate is no longer able to be pushed with just a finger, so you really have to put some force to move the stone now. Ed used to say, "I know the secret of how the pyramids of Egypt were built!" These were not just idle words as Ed displayed his knowledge in every aspect of the building of Coral Castle. No one else has ever been able to explain how he built Coral Castle or to recreate what Ed had done.

A man named Jeremy Stride successfully deciphered the numbers that Ed had put on the wall at Coral Castle. These numbers were a clue to the magnetic flywheel or electromagnetic generator that Ed made to help him build his castle. Jeremy Stride made a video called "Code 144" to explain how the numbers 7129 and 6105195 fit into the pattern of the magnetic flywheel. He divided up the degree circle into 15 degree intervals just like the Song of Degrees hint with the 15 chapters. Then he put the sums of prime numbers around the circle too, and they lined up to certain degrees on the circle.

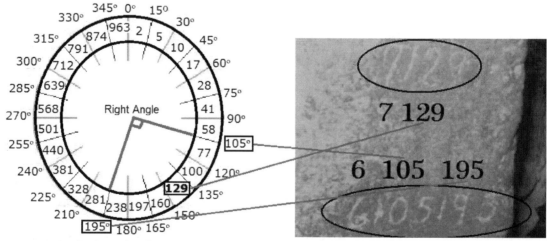

The outer circle displays the degrees around a circle at 15 degree intervals. The inner circle displays the sum of prime numbers.

Ed's Numbers on the Wall

Ed also used English gematria in his work, which shows that he knew about the English gematria code that was hidden in the King James Version of the Bible. He used Pythagorean math to reduce every letter to a single digit number. He encoded English gematria into his admission box, so that "ADM." is 144, and that number is in Revelation 21. He also encoded the number 21 in the addition of the letters of "ED.L.", which he displayed in a photo. Another interesting coincidence or not is that he used "U" magnets going around his flywheel and the letter U in English gematria is 21.

ADM. IS 144

A=1	J=10	S=19	1
B=2	K=11	T=20	2
C=3	L=12	U=21	3
D=4	M=13	V=22	4
E=5	N=14	W=23	5
F=6	O=15	X=24	6
G=7	P=16	Y=25	7
H=8	Q=17	Z=26	8
I=9	R=18		9

English Alphabet Code

ED.L 5+4+12=21

Another interesting connection comes from John 21, which is also using Ed's 21 codes. I was reading the verses about the fishing story one day and the sea of Tiberias leaped out at me for a reason. In John 21:1 it says "*After these things Jesus shewed himself again to the disciples at the **sea of Tiberias**; and on this wise shewed he himself*". I thought maybe I need to add up the letters, since the whole fishing story takes place at this location. I didn't follow through on my thought until the next day, so I added them up and it came to 129.

Sea of Tiberias
19+5+1+15+6+20+9+2+5+18+9+1+19= 129

At first, I didn't get the significance, because I thought it would add up to 153. Then I thought about it awhile and realized that this could be one of the numbers on the degree circle. I checked it out and it was one of the sums of primes. It was one of the numbers that Ed highlighted on the wall at Coral Castle. I also did a little math and found out that if subtract 129 from 153 that the sum is 24, which this is the amount of sections around the degree circle and the number of magnets that Ed used on his flywheel.

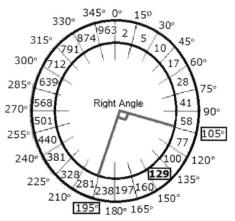

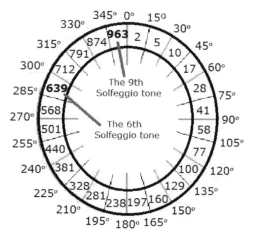

The outer circle displays the degrees around a circle at 15 degree intervals. The inner circle displays the sum of prime numbers.

The outer circle displays the degrees around a circle at 15 degree intervals. The inner circle displays the sum of prime numbers.

After watching Jeremy Stride's code 144 video, I also noticed that 2 of the Solfeggio tones were in the sums of prime numbers. This shows that somehow the Solfeggio tones were used in the building of Coral Castle and many researchers have suggested that Ed used harmonic sound waves to move the stones.

Ed's blueprint for his magnetic flywheel comes from many different places in the Bible. We can see that he divided up the degree circle into 15 degree intervals, and that clue comes from the Song of Degrees in Psalms 120-135. In the Solfeggio tones chapter I showed that the 15 chapters are a clue to break down the degree circle into 24 sections with the 15 degree intervals. The next clue to the 129 in the flywheel came from John 21 as I have already shown. Most of the clues of Ed's flywheel come from Revelation 4, which tells us about the throne of God and describes it in every detail. When looking at Ed's flywheel I noticed that it was matching the throne of God and the more I looked the more that I found that this had to have been his blueprint. He had the 24 magnets going around the flywheel, which were the 24 elders. In Revelation 4:4 it says *"And round about the throne were four and twenty seats: and upon the seats I saw **four and twenty elders** sitting, clothed in white raiment; and they had on their heads crowns of gold"*. He also had 4 rods with 4 round pieces going around the inside, which I quickly realized are the 4 beast surrounding the throne of God. In Revelation 4:6 it said, *"And before the throne there was a sea of glass like unto crystal: and in the midst of the throne, **and round about the throne, were four beasts** full of eyes before and behind"*. Those are two things in

106

Ed's flywheel that are similar to the throne of God, but still there was more evidence that I have found. In the middle of the flywheel are a handle and six holes that are in the shape of the Star of David. This is another feature that is encoded in Revelation 4 for the throne of God. In Revelation 4:8 the verse says, "*And the four beasts had each of them six wings about him; and they were full of eyes within: and they rest not day and night, saying, Holy, holy, holy, LORD God Almighty, which was, and is, and is to come*". The six wings are referring to the six vertices or triangles on outside of the hexagon, so this verse is showing the pattern of the Star of David. Another clue is given in the words of "holy, holy, holy", which are really an English gematria code. The word holy adds up to 60, and an equilateral triangle has 60 degree angles on its vertices. There are 3 vertices and sides on a triangle, so this is why the word holy is repeated 3 times.

$$H=8 \quad O=15 \quad L=12 \quad Y=25 \quad 8+15+12+25=60$$

The eyes within are clearly visible in the picture below and they are the heads on the ends of each of the U magnets. Ed left each of them exposed and did not cement over the metal, so they are left sticking through. We can see that Ed Leedskalnin carefully followed all of the clues that were encoded within Revelation 4 and also clues in other books of the Bible, as well.

Following the blueprint pattern being presented in Revelation 4, I started to notice that Ed left a clue as to what needs to be added to the flywheel. Upon looking at the picture of the Star of David in the moon pool, I realized that this was a major clue to the magnetic flywheel, so I started to look for more pictures of the flywheel to see if there was a container for water within the wheel. To my amazement the flywheel did seem to have a bowl like area that could contain water. In Revelation 4:6 it says that "before the throne there was a sea of glass like unto crystal" and Ed's moon pool shows water around the Star of David. The Star of David in the center of the flywheel shows the connection to add water, which would be like a sea of glass and the crystal analogy is showing the face of water is hexagonal. Water must be the key to making the flywheel work, and it's interesting that the water in that bowl will touch the head of the U magnet that Ed left exposed in the cement.

Rev. 4:6 *And before the throne there was a **sea of glass** like unto crystal: and in the midst of the throne, and round about the throne, were **four beasts full of eyes** before and behind.*

Ed's magnetic flywheel produced electricity and it's sometimes called an electromagnetic generator. The interesting attribute to the throne of God in Revelation 4 is that it produced lightning and sound. In Revelation 4:5 it says, "*And **out of the throne proceeded lightnings and thunderings and voices**: and there were seven lamps of fire burning before the throne, which are the seven Spirits of God*". As I already discussed in Numbers 21, the fiery serpent is referring to lightning or electricity, so we know that one of the goals of the throne of God is to produce electricity and Ed's flywheel was reported to produce electricity. In Revelation 4:5 it says that there were seven lamps burning before the throne, and it calls them the seven Spirits of God, and I already explained that this is the seven forms of the electromagnetic spectrum.

Another interesting feature of Ed's numbers on the wall and the degree circle that he used to make his flywheel is that the numbers also fit in with the John 21 story. Jeremy Stride hypothesizes that a pyramid was positioned on top of the flywheel, and that Ed's numbers on the wall show where to position the pyramid. One of the corners on the base is positioned at the sums of prime numbers for number seventeen. It's interesting how that number keeps coming up over and over again. The number 17 must be implying that the fishing net is electromagnetic. Also, another position of the base is at the 129 number which was encoded into the John 21 story.

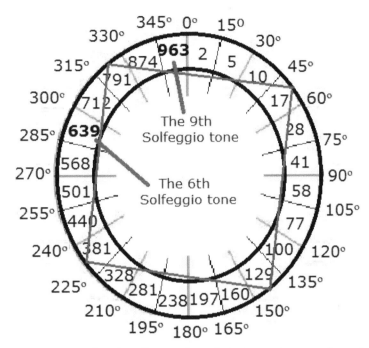

The outer circle displays the degrees around a circle at 15 degree intervals. The inner circle displays the sum of prime numbers.

While the fiery serpent on the pole healed people, the ark killed people and was taken many times into battle. The Ark of the Covenant was considered to be very dangerous at times and seems to be a more powerful electrical device than the fiery serpent on the pole and the throne of God. In 2 Samuel 6, Uzzah tried to steady the ark after the oxen shook it, and he was instantly killed, and in 1 Samuel 6:19 there were over 50,000 men that were killed just for looking inside of the ark. Out of the three electrical devices that were mentioned in the Bible, the Ark of the Covenant was the only device that was used as a weapon in wars.

A documentary called "The Ark of the Covenant Revealed" recreated a model of the ark to do an experiment to see if it was possible for an electrical arc to be emitted between the Cherubim on top of the ark. David Hutchinson successfully proved that the Ark of the Covenant is an electrical device and the arc of light burned for a little bit. The experiment was unable to reproduce the ark out of gold, and so they substituted copper to prove it would arc; however after a few minutes, it burst into flames. The experiment was successful although I can't help but wonder what it would have been like had they used gold as their plating for the ark.

It's surprising to think that the Bible gives blueprints to electrical devices, and I can't imagine what else the Bible could encode as far as revealing the technological knowledge of the ancient people. Most people are not aware of the technological aspects of the Bible, instead preferring to think of the ancient people as being primitive. But I often wonder who are the primitive people, as of yet mankind still can not duplicate the Great Pyramid and various other archeological curiosities. Ed Leedskalnin offered us a glimpse of the ancients, as he sought to replicate some of their technologies in our modern age. He showed us that there isn't anything new under the sun, and he showed us that the Bible has blueprints that could truly help mankind if we would just open our eyes and study the words before us. Ed never told anyone how he built his castle, but when I compared his magnetic flywheel to the throne of God, it matched the blueprint in every way. Some people believe that Ed took his secrets with him when he died, but I believe that all of his secrets were left behind at Coral Castle and in the Bible. I believe the Bible has the solution to the technology of using a clean energy source. Who would ever believe that the Bible could contain the solutions to all of the problems of mankind, but it does.

"Important lessons about our environment have come from spacecraft missions to the planets — by exploring other worlds we safeguard this one. By itself I think this fact more than justifies the money our species has already spent sending ships to other worlds. It is our fate to live during one of the most perilous, and at the same time one of the most hopeful, chapters in human history... The same rocket and nuclear and computer technology that sends our ships past the farthest known planet can also be used to destroy our global civilization. Exactly the same technology can be used for good and evil."
- Carl Sagan *Cosmos (episode #13 update)

The Bible is an encyclopedia galactica of useful information for mankind. It has significantly shaped our moral behavior with the Ten Commandments and other laws to help us become an ethical society. At a time, where modern society has progressed to a point of technological and scientific advancements, we find that we stand on the brink of utter destruction. We as a human civilization are in a very fragile bubble right now, and we stand at the crossroads of either transformation or destruction. I can remember watching Cosmos in the eighth grade as Carl Sagan talked about the perilous times that we are living within right now. He talked about nuclear weapons and pollution as well as various other problems that mankind are having to face in this infancy of a technological society, and he talked about if we would be able to make it past this tumultuous time of trouble. The Bible tells us that we can indeed make it past this destructive phase that we are in right now, and not only that but the Bible shows us that there are clean sources of energy that can be taken from the electromagnetic energies all around us. This is a free source of energy and people like Nikola Tesla and Ed Leedskalnin developed these technologies that are presented to us in the Bible. Humankind is in its technological infancy and we are either capable of improving mankind or destroying it. Do we turn to our Creator for the answers, or do we rely on ourselves? The only way to overcome this volatile time that we are living in right now is to follow all of the blueprints that God and Jesus Christ have given to us. Are we listening?

RHESUS BLOOD TYPES

Genesis 3:15 And I will put enmity between thee and the woman, and between thy seed and her seed; it shall bruise thy head, and thou shalt bruise his heel.

The Bible very quickly tells us right after the creation story that there are two different seeds. Many people fail to recognize this fact that is being presented to us in Genesis 3:15, but clearly we are being told that there are two different species. The word seed in the Bible can refer to human seed or offspring, and it can refer to planting God's word. In Genesis 3:15, we are being told that Satan and God have their own seed or species on the planet Earth. It's interesting about the verse number for this verse, as I have already covered in the chapter on the number 153 that there is a relationship between 153 and 666. I showed that the 153 triangle is God's and Jesus Christ sign and that the 666 triangle represents Satan's mark of the beast. Another interesting thing about the 153 number is that the sum of the cube of those three numbers adds up to 153.

This verse number seems to be hinting around about the number 153, which is the number for the Israelite and grail bloodline. Another interesting thing is that the verse number also hints around about Satan's seed or the serpent bloodline, as it is sometimes called. There is a phenomenon that comes from adding the different combinations of the numbers 1, 3 and 5.

THE DIFFERENT COMBINATIONS OF THE NUMBERS 1, 3 & 5

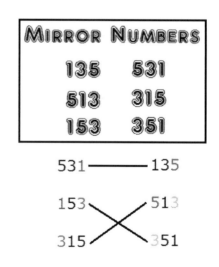

666 PATTERN

531 + 135 = 666
153 + 513 = 666
315 + 351 = 666

531   135
153   513
315   351

2 WRAPAROUND SEQUENCES

MIRROR NUMBERS

135   531
513   315
153   351

531——————135
153   513
315   351

We can see that the different combinations of the 1, 3 and 5 numbers added together as 3 pairs will add up to the beast number of 666. It's interesting that this verse from Genesis 3:15 is encoding another mathematical phenomenon that occurs between the 153 and 666 number. Remember the 666 and 153 triangle's perimeters added together is the sum of 153. These number patterns display both seeds in a clever and interactive way.

In the graphic on page 110, you can see on the left side that there is a wraparound effect in this pattern of numbers. On the right side you can see that one of the addition pairs that add up to 666 has two mirror numbers, and the other two addition pairs are not mirror numbers. I drew a line to show which mirror numbers go together. I noticed that my lines formed a subtraction and multiplication symbols and thought that this is a kooky coincidence. I decided to subtract the same numbers and the first sum I got back was a Solfeggio tone.

$$531-135 = 396$$
$$513-153 = 360$$
$$351-315 = 36$$

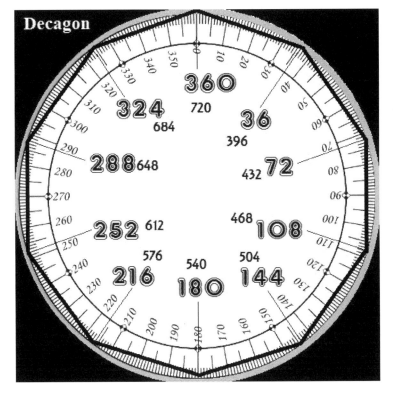

36

72

108 Solfeggio skip rate

144 Rev. 21:17

180

216

252

288

324 Solfeggio tone triplet skip rate

360 Degrees in a circle

396 3rd Solfeggio tone

432 Solfeggio tone triplet skip rate

These numbers show another pattern that can be fully explored in the degree circle. The number 360 came up second, and that is the amount of degrees in a circle, and then 36 showed up on the third line, so I took the clue to divide up the degree circle into 36 degree intervals. I did two rounds to show the 3rd Solfeggio tone, which lines up with the number 36. Two of the Solfeggio tone triplet skip rate numbers came up as well. What amazed me the most is that the 36 degree interval traces out the pattern of our DNA as a decagon, and remember the inside angles are at 144 degrees, and the outside angles are at 36 degrees. These number patterns keep coming up over and over again. The numbering of the verse has taken us back to the Solfeggio tones in this pattern, and 144,000 Israelites will sing the new song with these tones. This verse is hinting around that God's seed will play a part in healing the people with this new song.

You may be wondering is there any evidence for these two seeds? On the surface we all look like the same humans….we all have the same organs, the same body type and we all have the same needs. There is one difference that has become really noticeable in these modern times, and it has to do with the blood. The word blood is used a lot in the Bible, and this is where we find the answers. There are 4 different blood types and they are O, A, B and AB. Now these four types really don't convey that there are two races or seeds, so we must look further. Looking further into the blood types is the key to finding two distinctly different blood types. The Rhesus blood type was discovered in 1937 by Karl Landsteiner and Alexander S. Wiener. They discovered that most people have the D antigen and protein on their red blood cells which is in common with the Rhesus monkeys; however, there are some people that do not have the D antigen and protein. People that have the D antigen are called Rhesus positive, and those without are called Rhesus negative.

Another interpretation of the two seeds could be referring to the Neanderthal and the Cro-Magnon people. The Neanderthal has been proven by geneticists to be a different species than modern humans. In the last few years the geneticists has said that Europeans and Asians could have about 1% to 4% of Neanderthal genetics. Neanderthal skeletons have been found in Europe and the Middle East, so two different species were around together in these areas.

The third interpretation of the two seeds has to do with an ancient myth that Eve had sex with Satan, and that their child was Cain. People that believe this interpretation call Cain's descendants the serpent bloodline and Seth's descendants became known as the Israelites. In Genesis 3:13 it says, *"And the LORD God said unto the woman, What is this that thou hast done? And the woman said, The serpent beguiled me, and I did eat"*. It's not hard to see that interpretation of the scriptures, when it is read from a sexual perspective. The serpent associated with Satan could very well be his phallus, and she was tempted to have a sexual relationship with him.

All of these interpretations and perspectives are valid, and I believe in keeping an open mind to all of them. Getting back to the scientific interpretation of the two seeds, the most valid proof is either in the Rhesus blood types or in the genetics. We find that the Neanderthal and Cro-Magnon (modern man) species have been proven by geneticists to be genetically different, so this is a scientific proof of two different seeds. Although, the date for these two species go way back further into prehistoric times than the timelines that biblical scholars are giving to the time frame of the Bible. We also find valid scientific proof for the two seeds in the two different Rhesus blood types. People have also debated over whether the Neanderthal had RH negative or RH positive blood and visa versa for the Cro-Magnon people.

In Genesis 6 we are told that the "*sons of God came in unto the daughters of men, and they bare children to them*". There have been all kinds of interpretations of this story. Some say that the fallen angels came down from Heaven and started having sexual relationships with humans, and others say it means that the two different seeds were mixing together. A popular modern day interpretation is that these gods or sons of gods were aliens that mated with humans and also genetically modified humans to be more like them. There is also a spiritual interpretation of this story where people believe it was believers in God mixing with non-believers.

In Daniel 2:43 it says, "*And whereas thou sawest iron mixed with miry clay, they shall mingle themselves with the seed of men: but they shall not cleave one to another, even as iron is not mixed with clay*". In this verse it talks about one of the seeds mixing with the other seed, and it also talks about how they will not cleave to one another. This verse seems to corroborate the interpretation that the two seeds are talking about the two Rhesus blood types. There are procreation problems that occur between RH negative women and RH positive men. A woman has a good chance of carrying her first born to birth, but any subsequent pregnancy has a high risk of miscarriages. This all changed with the development of $Rh_o(D)$ Immune Globulin to prevent hemolytic disease of a newborn, which was causing miscarriages and blue babies to be born. Prior to 1968, RH negative women had miscarriages if the baby was RH positive. The antibodies in a RH negative woman will actually attack the baby like it is a virus, because these two blood types do not mix. The problem with RH negative pregnancies certainly suggests that one seed does not cleave with the other seed just as the Bible says in Daniel 2:43.

The problems with the RH negative blood mixing with the RH positive blood go further than just the procreation problems. Jessica Farrell and many other researchers have found a connection between auto-immune problems and those that are of mixed heritage. Most of the RH negatives blood types are of mixed heritage or what we would call hybrids. I am B RH negative, but both of my parents are RH positives. My parents have alleles that are mixed, and so they are considered to be RH negative carriers, which means that they have alleles that are both positive and negative (+,-). They have genetics for both blood types, and they both gave me their RH negative alleles.

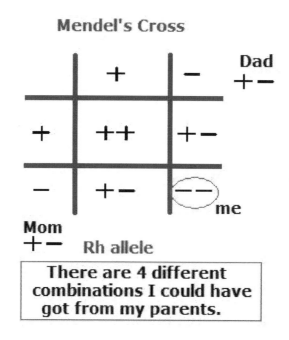

Mendel's Cross

There are 4 different combinations I could have got from my parents.

As you can see from the Mendel's cross up above, I had a 25% chance of being RH positive, a 50% chance of being a RH negative carrier (RH positive) and a 25% chance of being RH negative. The RH positive blood type is dominant and the RH negative blood type is recessive, so most of the hybrid or mixed blood is RH negative. In the hybrid bloodlines, the RH negative blood type only pops out rarely here or there. In Europe and America the RH negative percentages are around 15% of the population, but in the world percentage of RH negatives, it is estimated to be around 7%.

Most of the RH negatives in the world are in Europe, Northern Africa, Ethiopia and the Middle East. The main RH negative zone is around the Mediterranean Sea area. Of course, any countries that were mainly settled by Europeans have a high percentage of the RH negative blood type, so this blood type has spread around the entire world in pockets here and there. Most biblical scholars say that the lost tribes of Israel and the tribe of Judah migrated all throughout Northern Europe and Northern Africa. Perhaps the Israelite and Jewish people can be better tracked by their blood type and not their religion.

In Daniel 2:43 the verse talks about how iron is mixed with clay, which is another hint to the two seeds. There is a lot of talk on the internet about how RH negatives have more copper in their blood than RH positives and that RH negatives have less iron and often become anemic. I can neither confirm nor deny that RH negatives have more copper or not, but I do know that I have had problems with anemia before. When looking at clay, I noticed that certain kinds of clay with iron look like the color of copper.

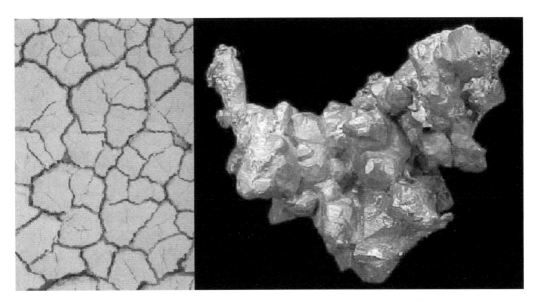

This appears to be a hint about the copper blood, so perhaps one seed has more iron in their blood, and the other seed has more copper. There is more evidence for this in the Bible with other copper connections. The Tabernacle and Temple used the metals of gold, silver and brass, which is an alloy of copper and tin in ancient times. The story of the brass serpent on the pole that healed the Israelite people is suggestive that the pure blood of the Israelite people before they mixed could be the RH negative copper blood. This blood does seem to have some interesting properties which make it healing. The RH negative blood can be given to RH positive people with no adverse effects, and this is why the O negative blood type is called the universal donor because it can be given to every blood type. Red Cross practically begs O negatives to donate their blood for this reason. There are reports that O negative blood is being used to help people that have the HIV virus known as AIDS. RH antibodies from O negative blood are being infused into HIV+/RH+ patients. The present inventors have found that RH antibodies delay the progression of infection with the Human Immunodeficiency (HIV), so this is being used as a treatment for AIDS. People with the RH negative blood type are known to have strong immune systems, and therefore they get sick less often than RH positive people.

The copper connection to the RH negative blood type is fascinating to me, because copper is conductive to electricity and therefore is used in wiring for electricity. Remember the brass serpent on the pole is representative of the fiery serpent that the Lord told Moses to put on the pole. As I already pointed out lightning or electrical arcs look like a serpent zig zagging back and forth, and it is fiery. This alone suggests that RH negatives have an electrical attribute to them, which means they could have an increased ability to work with electromagnetic energy. In fact, one of the characteristics often associated with RH negatives is that they have the ability to disrupt electrical devices. This is another reason why God calls his people the elect, because the first syllable in **elect**ricity is elect. I wrote more about this topic in my book "The Levite Priest and the RH negative Blood type", so if you would like to learn more then read this book for more evidence that the RH negative blood type is an Israelite and Jewish blood type.

An interesting side note to all of this has to do with the myth of a grail bloodline, which is most often nowadays associated with the idea that Jesus Christ and Mary Magdalene married and had children together. Most people are not aware of the perspective that the Statue of Liberty that was given to us by France could be symbolic of Mary Magdalene and the grail bloodline. It is interesting and perhaps ironic that the Statue of Liberty is made out of copper. This could perhaps be another clue to the grail bloodline that has settled in America.

I was contacted by another RH negative researcher named Angellica Goodson-Lord who has written several books on the subject. She believes that there are two kinds of RH negative people: one that has the copper blood and one that does not. She believes that the copper blood comes from the aliens/fallen angels that mixed with humans. This is totally a whole different perspective, and it leads to another interpretation of the two seeds. In this interpretation the two seeds could both have RH negative blood, and only one has copper based blood and the other does not.

In Daniel 2, Nebuchadnezzar has many dreams and one is about a mysterious statue made of many different metals. It says in Daniel 2:32-33, "*32 This image's head was of fine gold, his breast and his arms of silver, his belly and his thighs of brass, 33 His legs of iron, his feet part of iron and part of clay*". It is explained by Daniel that these are five different kingdoms and the statue shows them in the image of a man. It's interesting that the feet are made of iron and clay, because in verse 40 we can find a connection to Genesis 3:15, which talks about the two seeds. In Daniel 2:40 it says, "*And the fourth kingdom shall be strong as iron: forasmuch as iron breaketh in pieces and subdueth all things: and **as iron that breaketh all these, shall***

it break in pieces and bruise".   In Genesis 3:15 it says that one seed will bruise the head and the other seed will bruise the heel. Now in Daniel 2:40 the scriptures are telling us that iron mixing with clay/copper will bruise the heel because the iron and clay are in the foot of the statue. Iron does not mix with clay very well, so we can see this as an analogy of the two seeds that do not mix and therefore it has weakened the Israelite bloodline. This is exactly what we see with the autoimmune and procreation problems between RH negatives and RH positives.

Daniel 2 Statue -15th century

Most biblical scholars interpret Genesis 3:15 as referring to Jesus Christ wounding the head of Satan, and Satan wounded the heel of Jesus. This scientific interpretation of blood types also shows that there is a problem between Satan's seed and God's seed mixing together. We can clearly see from verse 40 in Daniel that the iron is bruising the heel of the copper blood people, so this aligns the copper blood with Jesus. Another story that shows that Jesus is connected with the copper blood is the brass serpent on the pole in Numbers 21. Jesus compares himself to the brass serpent in John 3:14, so not only can we see that copper blood heals the people, but also that Jesus must have had copper blood as well.

As I said before, copper is an electrical conductor and electricity looks like the fiery serpent of lightning, so it is interesting that Jesus is said to return back to Earth like lightning for the second coming. In Matthew 24:27 it

119

says, "*For as the **lightning** cometh out of the east, and shineth even unto the west; so shall also the coming of the Son of man be*". In Revelation 4:5 it says that lightning came out of the throne of God, and in Revelation 5:6 we learn that the Lamb is in the midst of the throne, which is Jesus Christ. We are always being shown a copper and lightning connection to Jesus Christ. From the Tabernacle with brass to the brass serpent on the pole, God and Jesus connect themselves with copper. It is also interesting to note that the net on the Bronze altar is also made out of brass and the RH negative people are said to have a copper based blood. In Exodus 27:4 it says, "*And thou shalt make for it a grate of **network of brass**; and upon the **net** shalt thou make four brasen rings in the four corners thereof*". I've made a theory a long time ago that Adam and Eve's descendants of the Israelite people are here to raise the vibration of this planet to prepare the earth for the harvest. The brass net represents what this bloodline is here to do, because the stories suggest that the brass serpent will heal the people, and that the brass net will be used for the fishing net of John 21. If God's seed represented the iron seed, than why would there be so much brass used in all of God's templates for the Tabernacle? I believe that God's seed has the copper blood, because many of the scriptures show the evidence.

Another thing that I noticed about Daniel 2:43 is that it shows a connection to the Solfeggio tones just like Genesis 3:15 did in the math code. The number 243 is a skip rate in the triplet numbers of the tones, so again we are being shown a connection for the Israelites to sing the new song.

In Daniel 2:39 it says, "And after thee shall arise another kingdom inferior to thee, and another **third kingdom of brass, which shall bear rule over all the earth**". This is another reference to the copper blood of the RH negatives. It is well known that the royals in Britain have the RH negative blood type and the grail bloodline is a royal one. The royal bloodlines are often called the bluebloods, and many RH negative researchers have pointed out that copper turns a bluish-green color when it oxidizes. Could bluebloods be an encoded word for the copper blood? I believe so. The book "Holy Blood, Holy Grail" by Michael Baigent, Henry Lincoln and Richard Leigh has some good research about the Holy Grail. They found that the word "sangraal" means Holy Grail in French, but if the word is divided in half it becomes "sang raal" or "sang real" in English, which means "blood royal" in French. The Holy Grail is said to be a cup that holds the blood of Jesus Christ, and Jesus came from the tribe of Judah, so he had the royal blood. The only way to carry royal blood is not in a cup, but in the womb. Jesus Christ and Mary Magdalene's offspring would have had the Holy Grail or royal blood. It's interesting that the words "sang raal" is called "sang real" in English, because those two words are suggestive of the Israelites and

Jews singing the new song in the last days. We can see from Daniel 2:39 that the kingdom of brass is referring to the royal bloodline of the tribe of Judah. This bloodline or seed mixed with the iron bloodline and in the statue of Nebuchadnezzar's dream, we see that after the iron and clay/copper mixed that God's seed was weakened or bruised in the heel as it says in Genesis 3:15. The hint of the Solfeggio tones in the math code of Genesis 3:15 and the hint of the tones in Daniel 2:43, shows that the new song of the 144,000 is crucial to fixing this problem and healing the Israelites. As Jesus said in John 3:14, we must raise or lift this brass serpent. The other hint in the cubing of the numbers of 1, 3 and 5 in Genesis 3:15 seem to be that we must raise this brass net.

As you can see, the scientific perspective of reading Genesis 3:15 as representing two different species that have two different Rhesus blood types makes perfect sense, but it could also be referring to the iron based blood versus the copper based blood. Daniel 2:43 has evidence that the copper blood mixed with the iron blood and was weakened, so in reading the Numbers 21 story from a prophetic point of view: we are told that we must raise the vibrations of the copper blood people to overcome and heal the Israelite people of their snake bites.

* Israelite- Is Real Light *

LEY LINES

Exodus 38:4 And he made for the altar a brasen grate of network under the compass thereof beneath unto the midst of it.

The definition of network is an arrangement of intersecting horizontal and vertical lines. The copper bloodline has spread all over the world, so it is interesting to consider that there is a network of lines all over our planet. There are the latitude and longitude lines all over the planet that creates a network of intersecting horizontal and vertical lines. The latitude and longitude lines were formed by the International meridian Conference in 1884. They settled on making the zero-longitude reference line in Greenwich of Britain, which helped to establish the time zones all over the world. There was however a more ancient network of lines that were established thousands of years ago, and we can see them by the positioning of ancient archeological sites from around the world. In Britain, standing stones, stone circles and mounds were erected along specific lines. The phrase ley line was coined by archaeologist Alfred Watkins in 1921 in his books "The Old Straight Track" and "Early British Trackways". These ley lines are considered to be areas where there is a strong electromagnetic energy. You can almost think of these ley lines as being like the nervous system of the Earth, much like our nervous system channels electrical impulses throughout our body, these ley lines channel the electrical impulses along the Earth.

The science of ley lines is considered by many to be pseudoscience, but I have found that there could be some evidence for this in the Bible. I suddenly started to get interested in ley lines last year, when I discovered that there was one near where I lived. This ley line is called the Arcadian Lei, but I have come to call it the Stonehenge ley line. It goes through Boston- MA, New York City- NY, Philadelphia- PA, Washington D.C., Pilot Mountain and Stone Mountain in the United States. It goes through Teotihuacan (Mexico City) in Mexico and right through Stonehenge in Britain. The most interesting place that it goes through is the Damascus and Mount Hermon area of Syria. It also goes through Turkey and close to the areas of the 7 churches in the book of Revelation.

My research in many different subjects has always had a weird way of connecting together like some vast spokes of an unseen wheel. So it was interesting that Stonehenge looks like a wheel of stone, and that it was connecting some of the most powerful and biggest cities in the world as well as a mountain that is mentioned in the Bible. It all started to make sense over time as I began to put the pieces of this very complex puzzle together. The key to the Stonehenge ley line seemed to be found in a mysterious mountain that has had some very unusual phenomenon and visitations in its ancient past.

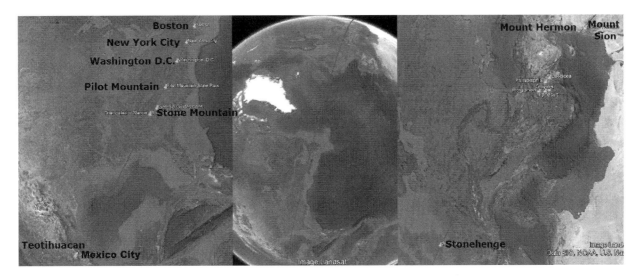

Mount Hermon's summit straddles the borders between Syria and Lebanon, and its southern slopes extend into the Israeli occupied portion of the Golan Heights. This mountain seems to have been a location point for the fallen angels or aliens that first came down to the Earth from the heavens. In the Book of Enoch at chapter 4 and verse 6 it says *"And they were in all two hundred; who descended in the days of Jared on the summit of Mount Hermon, and they called it Mount Hermon, because they had sworn and bound themselves by mutual imprecations upon it"*. The Book of Enoch tells basically the same story as Genesis 6 but it elaborates quite a bit more than what the Bible does. In the Bible the sons of God came down to be with women, but in the book of Enoch it calls them angels. In Enoch 4:2 it says, *"And the angels, the children of the heaven, saw and lusted after them, and said to one another: 'Come, let us choose us wives from among the children of men and beget us children"*. The Book of Enoch pretty much tells us the location of where this first took place on the earth and it just so happens that this energy ley line goes right through this area. Was this the scene of a first contact scenario between humans and space aliens, or were they really angels that had descended from a higher dimension?

I recently learned this year that Mount Hermon is actually Mount Sion in the Bible. As it said in the book of Enoch, the angels named it Mount Hermon, but God had a different name for this mountain. In Deuteronomy 4:48 it says, *"From Aroer, which is by the bank of the river Arnon, even unto mount*

Sion, which is Hermon". This verse says that Mount Hermon is Mount Sion, and this Sion is not to be confused with Mount Zion of Jerusalem. It's interesting that another verse actually describes Mount Sion of being a place of angels. In Hebrews 12:22 it says, "But ye are come unto mount Sion, and unto the city of the living God, the heavenly Jerusalem, and to an innumerable company of angels". That verse seems to confirm that this mountain is associated with the angels in ancient times. I find it really interesting that this mountain is very significant in so many different ways, but the most special thing that could have happened there seems to be completely erased from the Bible, and I wonder why. It turns out that Jesus was preaching very close to this mountain at around the time that he transfigured. He had been preaching in Caesarea Philippi just prior to the transfiguration on a mountain that is unnamed, and on Google Earth I measured the distance between Mount Hermon and Caesarea Philippi, and it was just 42 miles away. It was just six days later that Jesus transfigured, so if we divide 42 by 6, then all he had to walk was 7 miles a day to be on top of Mount Hermon. That is completely possible, and so I believe that Mount Hermon is the place of the transfiguration, although many believe the site to be at Mount Tabor. If you campare Mount Tabor to Mount Hermon/Sion, then you will see that Mount Tabor looks like a hill. In Matthew 17:1 we are told *"And after six days Jesus taketh Peter, James, and John his brother, and bringeth them up into an high mountain apart"*. This verse says that he brought them to a high mountain and not to a hill, so Mount Hermon has to be the location of the transfiguration.

The Tabernacle latitude and longitude coordinates lining up with the Roseline or Paris meridian is further proof that Mount Sion is where Jesus transfigured, since it lines up 33.33 degrees both for the latitude and the longitude. This mountain also will be where the 144,000 will be with Jesus Christ in the last days. In Revelation 14:1 it says, *"And I looked, and, lo, a Lamb stood on the mount Sion, and with him an hundred forty and four thousand, having his Father's name written in their foreheads"*.

The new song of the 144,000 is to be sung with the tones found in Numbers 7, and the 144,000 will sing this song together on Mount Sion with Jesus Christ. The Tabernacle latitude and longitude coordinates are positioned in a place to mark the Roseline or Paris Meridian and the Stonehenge ley line also marks Mount Sion. The angle of the Stonehenge ley line is a clue to use the Solfeggio tones on Mount Sion, and all throughout this energetic ley line. I noticed that the circle around Stonehenge is a perfect circle, so I got the clue to measure the angle of the Stonehenge line on Google Earth, and to my amazement a significant number in the skip rate of the Solfeggio tones came up. After seeing that number, I thought maybe Stonehenge should be called toneshenge, because the stone and tones anagram is used all throughout the Bible. The angle of the Stonehenge ley line is 108 degrees, and that is in the skip rate of the tones.

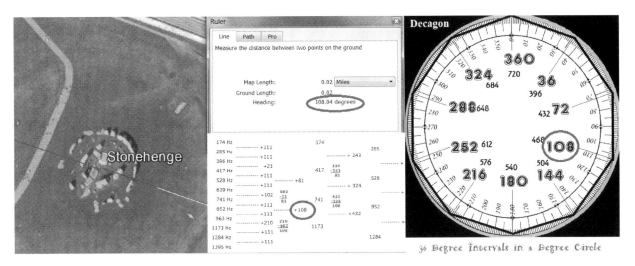

36 Degree Intervals in a Degree Circle

The 108 number is not only a skip rate number in Solfeggio tones math, but is also the angle inside a pentagon and an angle in the 36 degree intervals of a degree circle. Remember the 36 degree interval hint was found in the 1, 3 and 5 mathematics clue, and the number 144 found in that pattern is a significant number for New Jerusalem in Revelation 21. Everything comes together perfectly with this Stonehenge ley line and Mount Sion, so we can see that the tones are to be used in conjunction with this ley line to help raise the vibrations of the planet Earth. We can almost see the ley line as the pole and the copper blooded Israelites raising the brass serpent on this pole or ley line. It's also ironic that Jesus' instruction for us to lift up the serpent on the pole is at John 3:14, which is the number of Pi. We know that the degree circle is the key to finding the tones to lift up the vibratory rate. Pi is the mathematical constant that is a ratio of a circle's circumference to its diameter and it is approximately 3.14159 or 3.14.

John 3:14 *And as Moses lifted up the serpent in the wilderness, even so must the Son of man be lifted up:*

This song will be used to change the world by lifting or raising the vibratory rate, and it will bring in the new Earth that is mentioned in Revelation 21. As I have shown, the numbers associated with the Solfeggio tones and skip rates have been encoded all throughout the Bible in many different places and in various kinds of ways. This is the tones for the song of the Lamb that is mentioned in Revelations **15:3**, which also displays the number of the fish that was caught in the net of John 21. In Revelation 15:3 it says, *"And they sing the song of Moses the servant of God, and the song of the Lamb, saying, Great and marvellous are thy works, Lord God Almighty; just and true are thy ways, thou King of saints"*.

There are three major peaks to Mount Hermon, and this too encodes the same message as the three pyramids of Giza in Egypt. Robert Bauval discovered that the three pyramids of Giza are in the shape of Orion's belt, and the Orion constellation is located in the Holy of Holies within the Tabernacle star map. In biblical times Orion was known to be a representation of the Messiah and Jesus Christ.

It gets even better than this with the Orion representation also being along the Stonehenge ley line in North America at Teotihuacan. This shows a direct line between the Teotihuacan area and the Mount Hermon area, so the Stonehenge ley line is connecting the 3 peaks of Mount Hermon with the 3 pyramids in Mexico and the 3 belt stars in the Orion Constellation in the sky.

TEOTIHUACAN, MEXICO   ORION'S BELT   PYRAMIDS OF GIZA, EGYPT

I put a line between the middle of Mount Hermon and the Great Pyramid to see how far they were apart, and it turned out to be 365 miles. My immediate reaction was that this can't be a coincidence because a solar year is 365 days. Someone that saw one of my You Tube videos about the measurement remarked that Enoch is said by many myths to be the builder of the Great Pyramid and he lived to be 365 years old. I found that to be amusing, as well. In Genesis 5:23 it says "*And all the days of Enoch were three hundred sixty and five years*". Perhaps this is a clue to the builder of the Great Pyramid and a clue to the solar years, but the interesting thing is that God's Mount Sion is connected to the pyramids of Giza by the 3 peaks of both.

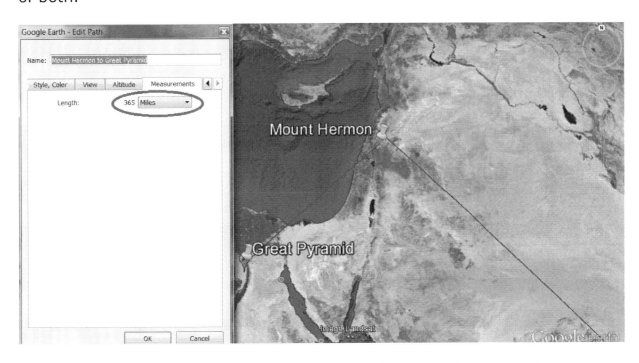

These ley lines are very strong and I have had the privilege to visit many places along the Stonehenge ley line and to connect with that energy and to play the Solfeggio tones. Wherever water and stones connect to these ley lines there is a tremendous amount of electromagnetic energy upon the Earth, and the vibrations of the planet Earth can be raised by the Solfeggio tones. I believe due to the patterns presented in the Bible in Numbers 21 and Revelation 21: that the energy of these ley lines travels in spirals. As the fiery serpent was raised on the pole, I believe raising the vibrations on the ley lines is like raising the serpent on the pole.

I was very blessed to meet a really good friend at Stone Mountain this year to carry out an experiment with the Solfeggio tones. Some very interesting things happened to us on the day we went up on the mountain to play our tones. It started lightning nearby after we got on top of the mountain, and so they said they would soon be closing down the tram, so that no one could come up or go down unless they hiked. We headed out onto the rock and tried to look for a certain location that I had found out about online, but we could not find it. This location was known as a triangulation disk, and it was made out of brass and had an equilateral triangle with a dot in the center. I had read online that the triangulation disk was surrounded by a circle in the rock that had 6 equidistant holes going around this circle. This is where I chose to play the tones, because it marked a central location on the rock dome. When we could not find it we simply just started playing the tones somewhere, but then we found out from my parents that there might be one more tram to take us down and we rushed back into the building. The last tram came up, and the woman operator told us that it was completely closed down for now, and she didn't know how long it would be closed. There were warnings from the speakers in the building that there was lightning in the area, and that everyone should just come off of the rock and wait safely in the building. My friend and I wanted to go back out on the rock to try to find the triangulation disk again, so we asked the tram operator, and she tried to tell us how to get there by saying it was in the middle of the rock. My son, my friend and I were heading out of the building as the warning broadcast was playing over the speakers, so while everyone was leaving the rock and heading into safety we were heading outside onto the rock to finish our mission. My friend and I were joking around and she remarked "Well, if it's our time to go, than it's our time to go". We showed no fear despite the lightning storms that surrounded Stone Mountain in every direction we could see. We started to search for the disk and each one of us spaced out to try and find this spot. We ended up going back to another bronze disk that we had found earlier, but this time I noticed the arrow on this disk. I had the thought to follow that arrow's direction, and so we headed out in the direction that the arrow was pointing. It almost seemed like we were following the directions of a treasure map. By following the arrow, we were able to find the triangulation disk and the circle that had 6 equidistant holes. We were only able to find 3 of the holes, as 3 of them seemed to have been cemented over. We sat inside of the circle that had the Star of David encoded. We did not think about the direction that we were facing, but we faced sitting east. We had been debating which direction we should face, so it was interesting that we didn't think about the direction at that time. It started to rain, but we still got the tablet out and played the tones. My friend was the only one that had brought an umbrella, so we used the green umbrella to protect the tablet. We played the 1122 Hz first and then the Holy Harmony song with the 9 main tones and the Christ chant of the Hebrew letters Yud Hey Shin Vav Hey. I also played the 24 tone Solfeggio, and Brian played the 24 tones as well. We had the mountain all to ourselves for quite awhile, because everyone else was in the building. Very shortly after playing the tones the rain ceased, and something quite amazing began to happen. The blue sky opened up above us, and all around the mountain in every direction was nothing but clouds. We could see rain in many different directions falling nearby, but Stone Mountain had beautiful blue skies overhead. Behind us was a monster storm of rain, and it kept looking like it might be heading our way, but it never did. My friend had the idea to put the crystals and gemstones I brought around the brass disk, so we put them all around. We played the tones for about an hour or more. There was a complete calmness or stillness in the air. At one point, I started to feel the energy within me. My friend commented that she was feeling a tingling sensation in her arm. At some point during the playing of the tones, I looked over and saw a security man watching us from just outside the building. No doubt, he must have been wondering why we didn't follow their warning to go inside the building. I read a little bit from the Song of Moses, and it kept talking about rain and rock, so it was a bit ironic.

Deuteronomy 32

*2 **My doctrine shall drop as the rain**, my speech shall distil as the dew, as the small rain upon the tender herb, and as the showers upon the grass:*

3 Because I will publish the name of the LORD: ascribe ye greatness unto our God.

*4 **He is the Rock**, his work is perfect: for all his ways are judgment: a God of truth and without iniquity, just and right is he.*

Another interesting piece of information that I found out about Stone Mountain is that the elevation is 1,686 feet (514 m) above sea level, and it is 825 feet (251 m) above the surrounding area. The 20th tone in the 24 scale of the Solfeggio tones is 825 Hz, so perhaps we should call this place Tones Mountain.

Matthew 8

24 And, behold, there arose a great tempest in the sea, insomuch that the ship was covered with the waves: but he was asleep.

25 And his disciples came to him, and awoke him, saying, Lord, save us: we perish.

26 And he saith unto them, Why are ye fearful, O ye of little faith? Then he arose, and rebuked the winds and the sea; and there was a great calm.

One lesson that I learned from our experiment at Stone Mountain on the Stonehenge ley line was that the Lord will calm the storms for us. If we are faithful and show no fear, we can accomplish great things. The three of us showed no fear, and we went out on the rock amidst a lightning storm to play our tones, and we were blessed to see the storm calm before us and the sunlight was able to shine through the dark clouds. The song of the Lamb can calm the mighty storms and lift us up on high, and all we have to do is trust in the Lord and his guidance.

* **Psalm 107:29** He maketh the storm a calm, so that the waves thereof are still.

GEMSTONES & CRYSTALS

Revelation 4:3 And he that sat was to look upon like a jasper and a sardine stone: and there was a rainbow round about the throne, in sight like unto an emerald.

In the Bible, the Levite high priest wore a gold breastplate with 12 gemstones, the throne of God is described with the rainbow colors of the gemstones and the foundations of the wall in the city of New Jerusalem is described as being garnished with 12 precious gemstones. A friend and I decided to experiment with gemstones and to learn all that we could learn about them. At first I set out to learn about the crystals, which come in many different gemstones. I learned that the quartz crystal is piezoelectric and pyroelectric, which means that they can produce electricity. Piezoelectric means that electricity resulting from pressure and pyroelectric means that a temporary voltage results when they are heated or cooled. It's interesting that a crystal is mentioned in Revelation 4:6 to be before the throne, as it specifically says *"before the throne there was a sea of glass like unto crystal"*. This verse ironically follows the verse that says *"out of the throne proceeded lightnings"*, which we know is electricity or the fiery serpent. After learning about the piezoelectric and pyroelectric properties of crystals, it was not hard to see a connection between the crystal and the lightning in the throne of God. In fact, a crystal radio is powdered by a quartz crystal, and crystals also resonate with a specific frequency.

It's interesting that scientists are now using crystals to store information or holograms by trapping light inside of crystals. They are doping the crystals with impurities so that they can trap the light within. In Discover magazine's April 2001 issue there is an article called "Trapping Light: This is the future, and it moves at 186,000 miles per second". This article covers the research of Eli Yablonovitch and Sajeev John, which after years of research were able to make a photonic crystal to store information. They used a face-centered cubic crystal to store information, because they found that it is the ideal crystal for capturing light. I find it quite ironic that the Bible also encodes the cube in the Holy of Holies and in New Jerusalem, as well as the Bible mentions the word crystal 5 times and 4 of those times is in conjunction with the throne of God. The 7 Spirits of God is also mentioned in connection with the throne of God, and as I have said before this is the 7 forms of the electromagnetic spectrum at which the center of the scale is visible light. The ancient words of the Bible seem to be encoding the special properties of crystals which are ideal in generating electrical currents and for storing information. This used to be stuff of science fiction and fantasy, but today it is a scientific reality that crystals can be used for some type of light data storage system.

An article from Britain's Mail Online website called "Superman 'memory crystals' to become a reality as scientists store computer data on powerful glass hard drive" shows just how far this new technology has gone. The article says that glass shards can store up to 50GB and will last thousands of years. It's unbelievable that crystals and glass are now being used to store information, and so I have to question is there a relevance to the Bible making references to glass and crystals amidst the lightning in the center of the throne of God. In Revelation 4:6 it clearly says that "before the throne there was a sea of glass like unto crystal", and now we have this modern day technology that is using crystal and glass for data storage systems, as well as crystals to power radios. Since the book of Revelation is a prophetic book, I think it is very easy to see a connection to our modern day computers. In Numbers 7, we were presented with the binary byte code, which is used in all of our modern day computers. And in the Solfeggio tones math we were shown patterns of binary and trinary numbers, so we are not only being shown the programming of our modern day computers, but perhaps the programming for the entire universe.

My friend sent me a link to a video about the 12 gemstones listed in Revelation 21, and the man on the video talked about the scientific properties of these gemstones. He said that all of the 12 gemstones are anisotropic, which means that if you shine cross polarized light through a thin sliver of the gemstone, then it will shine with the colors of the rainbow. Other gemstones such as diamonds and rubies show up as black underneath a microscope when you shine cross polarized light through them.

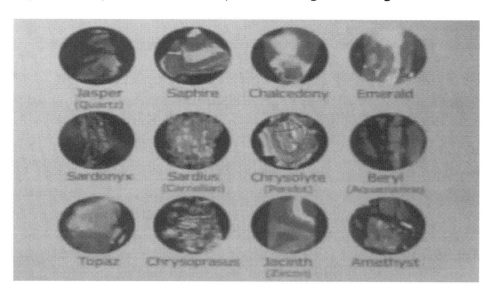

In Revelation 4:3 it says, "*And he that sat was to look upon like a jasper and a sardine stone: and there was a rainbow round about the throne, in sight like unto an emerald*". This verse is hinting around about the rainbow effect of the anisotropic gemstones, because all three gemstones listed in this verse are also mentioned in Revelation 21.   It is also hinting around about the rainbow colors of the Solfeggio tones, as well, so there is a dual meaning here.

God builds New Jerusalem with very precious gemstones, and He had his high priest wear 12 gemstones on their golden breastplate. As you can see from the latest scientific knowledge about gemstones and crystals, God put them here for a reason and it goes far beyond the concepts of adornments of jewelry or beyond monetary investments. Gemstones and crystals may be beautiful and profitable, but being able to store information within a crystal for thousands of years is priceless.

APPENDIX

I decided to put my graphics that I didn't use in the chapters of this book in this appendix for references.

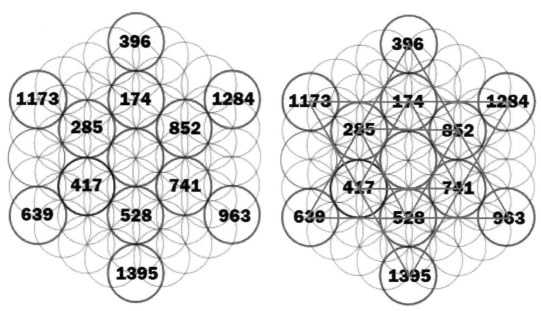

12 TONE SOLFEGGIO SCALE IN METATRON'S CUBE

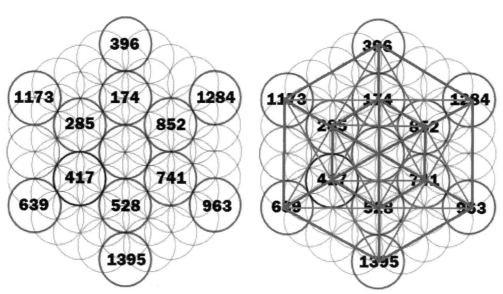

12 TONE SOLFEGGIO SCALE IN METATRON'S CUBE

This is an excerpt from an article I wrote for my mom's book "Roots of a Hillbilly Family from West Virginia". The ley line that goes through

Stonehenge to Mount Sion, also shows where the tribe of Judah and some Israelites migrated.

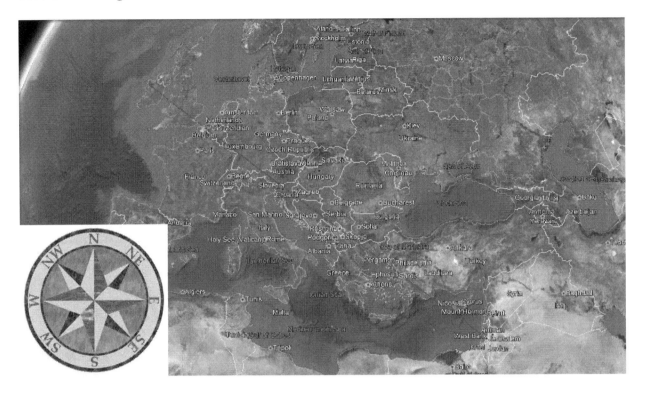

Isaiah 49:12 *Behold,* ***these shall come from far: and, lo, these from the north and from the west;*** *and these from the land of Sinim.*

"Take a map of Europe. Lay a line due northwest of Jerusalem across the continent of Europe, until you come to the sea, and then to the islands in the sea! This line takes you directly to the British Isles!" –Herbert W. Armstrong (The United States and Britain in Prophecy)

Furthermore, Armstrong offers further proof from the Bible that hints around about Israel being on islands. God refers to Israel as isles, on the same chapter where he talks about the tribe of Judah moving to a new place from the directions of the north and the west. The British Isles are exactly northwest from Jerusalem in Israel.

Isaiah 49

1 Listen, ***O isles,*** *unto me; and hearken, ye people, from far; The LORD hath called me from the womb; from the bowels of my mother hath he made mention of my name.*

2 And he hath made my mouth like a sharp sword; in the shadow of ***his hand hath he hid me,*** *and made me a polished shaft; in his quiver hath he hid me;*

3 And said unto me, ***Thou art my servant, O Israel,*** *in whom I will be glorified.*

There are other verses that also describe Israel as being in the isles or islands, as well.

Jeremiah 31:9-10 *⁹ They shall come with weeping, and with supplications will I lead them: I will cause them to walk by the rivers of waters in a straight way, wherein they shall not stumble: for I am a father to Israel, and Ephraim is my firstborn.*

*¹⁰ Hear the word of the LORD, **O ye nations, and declare it in the isles afar off, and say, He that scattered Israel** will gather him, and keep him, as a shepherd doth his flock.*

Isaiah 41:1

*41 Keep silence before me, **O islands**; and let the people renew their strength: let them come near; then let them speak: let us come near together to judgment.*

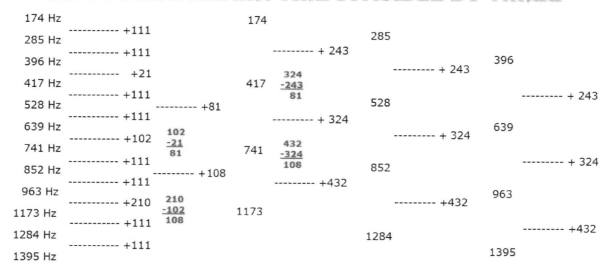

Solfeggio Tones: 174/3=58, 285/3=95, 396/3=132, 417/3=139, 528/3=176, 639/3=213, 741/3=247, 852/3=284, 963/3=321, 1173/3=391, 1284/3=428, 1395/3=465

Skip Rates: 111/3=37, 21/3=7, 102/3=34, 210/3=70, 81/3=27, 108/3=36, 243/3=81, 324/3=108, 432/3=144

All of the Solfeggio tones are divisible by three, which gives extra meaning to the trinity and to the number three being encoded into the John 21 story several times.

MATH OF THE SKIP NUMBERS

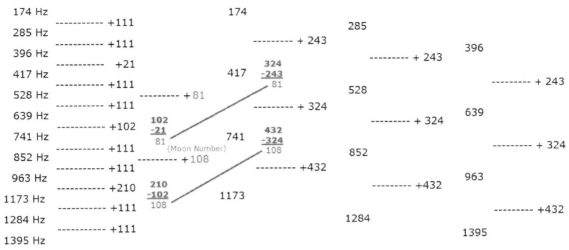

174 Hz
---------- +111
285 Hz
---------- +111
396 Hz
---------- +21
417 Hz
---------- +111
528 Hz
---------- +111
639 Hz
---------- +102
741 Hz
---------- +111
852 Hz
---------- +111
963 Hz
---------- +210
1173 Hz
---------- +111
1284 Hz
---------- +111
1395 Hz

174

285
--------- + 243
396
--------- + 243
417   324
      -243
       81
      --------- + 324
528
639
--------- + 324
741   432
      -324
       108
(Moon Number)   --------- +432
852
--------- +432
963

1173
1284
1395

--------- + 243

--------- + 243

--------- + 324

--------- + 324

--------- +432

--------- +432

102
-21
81

210
-102
108

852 --------- +108

All skip numbers are divisible by three.   111/3=37 **21**/3=7 102/3=**34** 210/3=70 & 243/3=81 324/3=108 432/3=**144**

Revelation 21:17 *And he measured the wall thereof, an hundred and forty and four cubits, according to the measure of a man, that is, of the angel.*

(Interesting notes: **17**X2=34 The numbers 21, 34 and 144 are Fibonacci numbers.   The skip rate skip numbers of 81 & 108 are divisible by 3 and 9.)

THE DIVINE NINE OF THE WINE

174 Hz
---------- +111
285 Hz
---------- +111
396 Hz
---------- +21
417 Hz
---------- +111
528 Hz
---------- +111
639 Hz
---------- +102
741 Hz
---------- +111
852 Hz
---------- +111
963 Hz
---------- +210
1173 Hz
---------- +111
1284 Hz
---------- +111
1395 Hz

174

285
--------- + 243
396
--------- + 243
417   324
      -243
       81
      --------- + 324
528
639
--------- + 324
741   432
      -324
       108
      --------- +432
852
--------- +432
963

1173
1284
1395

--------- + 243

--------- + 243

--------- + 324

--------- + 324

--------- +432

--------- +432

102
-21
81

210
-102
108

--------- + 81

--------- +108

243/9=27 324/9=36 432/9=48 81/9=9 108/9=12
396/9=44 639/9=71 963/9=107 1395/9=155

THE NUMBER 432

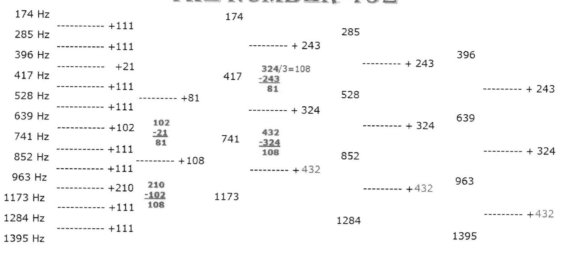

"By detuning the note 'a' to 432 (harmonic of 54, 108 & 25,920 / 60) then the frequency of 'D' becomes 144 hz (144000 cycles per second) Using 432 hz as frequency allows for all the wavelengths to harmonize easily with each other." http://www.tumblr.com/tagged/432%20hz

The number 25,920 is the precession of the equinox cycle. (25,920/60=432) The number 108 is the Moon number. The Moon reflects the light of the Sun and the 144,000 reflect the Light of the SON. The number 144 is the number for light, and the number 144,000 is the grid speed of light on the Earth of 144,000 minutes of arc per grid second. (432/3=144)

The precession of the equinox cycle is displayed within the numbers of Solfeggio math. One precession cycle last 25,920 years and the number 432 is a multiple of 25,920.

THE NUMBERS 108, 111 & 210 IN THE SKIP RATES

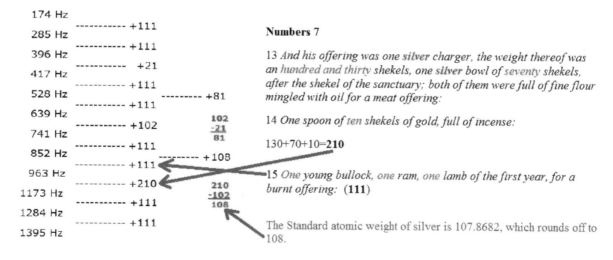

Numbers 7

13 *And his offering was one silver charger, the weight thereof was an hundred and thirty shekels, one silver bowl of seventy shekels, after the shekel of the sanctuary; both of them were full of fine flour mingled with oil for a meat offering:*

14 *One spoon of ten shekels of gold, full of incense:*

130+70+10=**210**

15 *One young bullock, one ram, one lamb of the first year, for a burnt offering:* **(111)**

The Standard atomic weight of silver is 107.8682, which rounds off to 108.

THE OTHER 12 SOLFEGGIO TONES

147 Hz
---------- +111   147
258 Hz   258
---------- +111   --------- + 324
369 Hz   --------- + 324   369
---------- +102
471 Hz   471   --------- + 324
---------- +111   --------- +81   --------- + 324
582 Hz   582
---------- +111   --------- + 243
693 Hz   693
---------- + 21   --------- + 243
714 Hz   714   --------- + 243
---------- +111   825
825 Hz   --------- +189
---------- +111   --------- +432
936 Hz   --------- +432   936
---------- +210   1146
1146 Hz   --------- +432
---------- +111   1257
1257 Hz   1368
---------- +111
1368 Hz

528 TRIANGLE

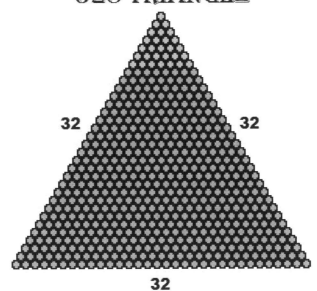

32   32

32

1+2+3+4+5+6+7+8+9+10+11+12+13+14+15+16+17+18+19+20+21+22+23+24+25+26+27+28+29+30+31+32=528

The 5th tone in the Solfeggio tones is 528 Hz and the number 528 is a triangle number.

139

Numbers 7

7 Two wagons and four oxen he gave unto the sons of Gershon, according to their service:

8 And four wagons and eight oxen he gave unto the sons of Merari, according unto their service, under the hand of Ithamar the son of Aaron the priest.

Number of bits	Number of values	2 raised to the power	Number of bytes	Unit	
1	2	1		Bit	0 / 1
2	4	2			
3	8	3			
4	16	4		Nibble	Hexadecimal unit
5	32	5			
6	64	6			64 codons in DNA
7	128	7			
8	256	8	1	Byte	One character
9	512	9			
10	1024	10			

What happens if we cube these numbers? To cube a number, just use it in a multiplication 3 times.

2^3 (2X2X2=8), 4^3 (4X4X4=64), 8^3 (8X8X8=512) See a pattern?

TRINARY & BINARY CODE IN THE SOLFEGGIO TONES

174 Hz		147 Hz	
	---------- +111		---------- +111
285 Hz		258 Hz	
	---------- +111		---------- +111
396 Hz		369 Hz	
	---------- +21		---------- +102
417 Hz		471 Hz	
	---------- +111		---------- +111
528 Hz		582 Hz	
	---------- +111		---------- +111
639 Hz		693 Hz	
	---------- +102		---------- +21
741 Hz		714 Hz	
	---------- +111		---------- +111
852 Hz		825 Hz	
	---------- +111		---------- +111
963 Hz		936 Hz	
	---------- +210		---------- +210
1173 Hz		1146 Hz	
	---------- +111		---------- +111
1284 Hz		1257 Hz	
	---------- +111		---------- +111
1395 Hz		1368 Hz	

Counting in Binary and Decimal

32	16	08	04	02	01		10	01	
					1			1	1
				1	0			2	2
				1	1			3	3
			1	0	0			4	4
			1	0	1			5	5
			1	1	0			6	6
			1	1	1			7	7
		1	0	0	0			8	8
		1	0	0	1			9	9
		1	0	1	0		1	0	10
		1	0	1	1		1	1	11
		1	1	0	0		1	2	12
		1	1	0	1		1	3	13
		1	1	1	0		1	4	14
		1	1	1	1		1	5	15
	1	0	0	0	0		1	6	16

BINARY # 14

1110

258
285
528
582
825
+852
3330

3330/3=1110

TRINARY CODE

000 001 002
010 011 012   21=7
020 021 022

100 101 102
110 111 112   102=11
120 121 122

200 201 202
210 211 212   210=21
220 221 222

Read more:
http://wiki.answers.com/Q/How_do_you_do_trinary_code#ixzz2IRRcb9yD

We use binary code in our computers. Binary code has also been used as a way to transmit information to extraterrestials. In 1972 binary code was used on the Pioneer 10 spacecraft and in 1974 it was transmitted into space as a message for ET's at Arecibo's radio telescope.

These numbers in Solfeggio math appear to be teaching us binary code, as well as trinary code.

#1. Trinary, or base 3, is a number system, just like our decimal system. Exept unlike the decimal system, trinary only uses 3 different digits: 0, 1, and 2.
http://howtodothat.wikidot.com/how-to-use-trinary-code

MATH OF THE TRIAD NUMBERS

FIRST 12 SOLFEGGIO TONES				**SECOND 12 SOLFEGGIO TONES** **BINARY # 14**			
444	**555**	**666**	**1284**	**888**	**1110**	**1332**	**2541**
174	285	396	1173	147	258	369	1146
417	528	639	1284	174	285	396	1173
+741	+852	+963	+1395	417	528	639	1257
1332	1665	1998	3852	471	582	693	1284
				714	825	936	1368
1332/3=444	1665/3=555	1998/3=666	3852/3=1284	+741	+852	+963	+1395
				2664	3330	3996	7623

(All numbers are divisible by 3 in Solfeggio math.)

2664/3=888   3330/3=1110   3996/3=1332   7623/3=2541

THE NUMBER 37

37 X 3 = 111 / 3	37 X 12 = 444 / 3	37 X 21 = 777 / 3	37 X 30 = 1110 / 3
37 X 6 = 222 / 6	37 X 15 = 555 / 6	37 X 24 = 888 / 6	37 X 33 = 1221 / 6
37 x 9 = 333 / 9	37 x 18 = 666 / 9	37 X 27 = 999 / 9	37 X 36 = 1332 / 9

FIRST 12 TONES

174 Hz	1+7+4=12=3
285 Hz	2+8+5=15=6 +
396 Hz	3+9+6=18=9 -
417 Hz	4+1+7=12=3
528 Hz	5+2+8=15=6 +
639 Hz	6+3+9=18=9 -
741 Hz	7+4+1=12=3
852 Hz	8+5+2=15=6 +
963 Hz	9+6+3=18=9 -
1173 Hz	1+1+7+3=12=3
1284 Hz	1+2+8+4=15=6 +
1395 Hz	1+3+9+5=18=9 -

YING   YANG

NEGATIVE
FEMALE
NIGHT
PASSIVE
MOON
INTUITIVE
COLD
SOFT

POSITIVE
MALE
DAY
ACTIVE
SUN
LOGICAL
HOT
HARD

6   9

SECOND 12 TONES

147 Hz	1+4+7=12=3
258 Hz	2+5+8=15=6 +
369 Hz	3+6+9=18=9 -
471 Hz	4+7+1=12=3
582 Hz	5+8+2=15=6 +
693 Hz	6+9+3=18=9 -
714 Hz	7+1+4=12=3
825 Hz	8+2+5=15=6 +
936 Hz	9+3+6=18=9 -
1146 Hz	1+1+4+6=12=3
1257 Hz	1+2+5+7=15=6 +
1368 Hz	1+3+6+8=18=9 -

ATOMS

NEUTRON:
LARGE WITH
NO CHARGE

PROTON:
LARGE WITH
POSITIVE CHARGE

ELECTRON:
SMALL WITH
NEGATIVE CHARGE

Proton
Neutron

Electron

FOUR STAR'S OF DAVID

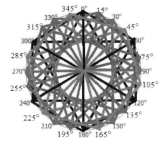

& FOUR HOLY OF HOLIES CUBES

Matthew 13:47

*Again, the kingdom of heaven is like unto a **net**, that was cast into the sea, and gathered of every kind:*

John 3:14   (It's interesting that this verse number is Pi.)

And as Moses lifted up the serpent in the wilderness, even so must the Son of man be lifted up:

John 21:11 *Simon Peter went up, and drew the net to land full of great fishes, an **hundred and fifty and three**: and for all there were so many, yet was not the net broken.*

The number 153 is a triangular number and a hexagonal number. Both the 153 equilateral triangle and the 153 hexagon are in this circular net.

π
3 . 14

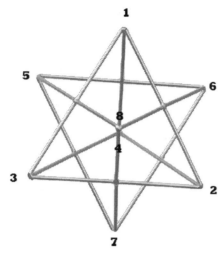

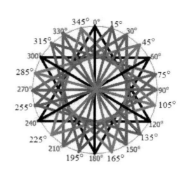

There are 32 vertices in 4 star tetrahedrons. The point in the middle of the star tetrahedrons would count as the 33rd point.

There are 8 vertices in 1 star tetrahedron.

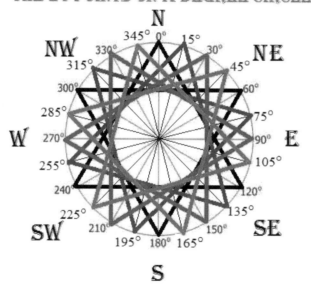

THE 24 POINTS ON A DEGREE CIRCLE

Black SOD is north and south.
Red SOD is east and west.
Blue SOD is northwest and southeast.
Green SOD is northeast and southwest.

Exodus 27:5

*And thou shalt put it under the **compass** of the altar beneath, that the **net** may be even to the midst of the altar.*

THE 24 POINTS ON A DEGREE CIRCLE

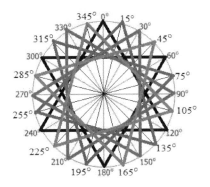

Rev. 4:8 And the four beasts had each of them six wings about him; and they were full of eyes within: and they rest not day and night, saying, Holy, holy, holy, Lord God Almighty, which was, and is, and is to come.

There are 4 Star of David's or beast used in this graphic, and each of the vertices is one of the 24 points or elders in the degree circle. Each Star of David contains 6 vertices or wings. The word Holy comes out to 60 in English gematria, and the Star of David is made up of 60 degree angles.

Could beast be an angram for beats?

In music and music theory, the **beat** is the basic unit of time, the pulse of the *mensural level*[1] (or *beat level*).[2] In popular use, the beat can refer to a variety of related concepts including: tempo, meter, rhythm and groove.

http://en.wikipedia.org/wiki/Beat_(music)

Could wings be an anagram for swing?

In music terms, the word "swing" refers to a bouncing groove that can be created in the rhythm of music.

http://blog.dubspot.com/swing-creative-use-of-groove-quantization/

FIRST 12 TONES — SECOND 12 TONES

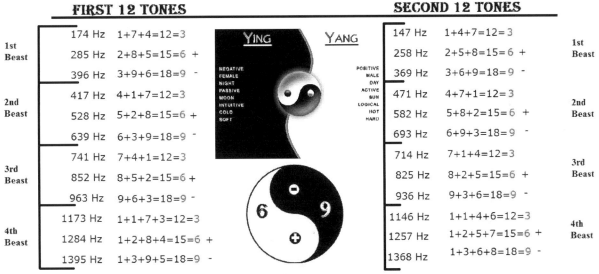

	First 12 Tones			Second 12 Tones		
1st Beast	174 Hz	1+7+4=12=3		147 Hz	1+4+7=12=3	1st Beast
	285 Hz	2+8+5=15=6 +		258 Hz	2+5+8=15=6 +	
	396 Hz	3+9+6=18=9 -		369 Hz	3+6+9=18=9 -	
2nd Beast	417 Hz	4+1+7=12=3		471 Hz	4+7+1=12=3	2nd Beast
	528 Hz	5+2+8=15=6 +		582 Hz	5+8+2=15=6 +	
	639 Hz	6+3+9=18=9 -		693 Hz	6+9+3=18=9 -	
3rd Beast	741 Hz	7+4+1=12=3		714 Hz	7+1+4=12=3	3rd Beast
	852 Hz	8+5+2=15=6 +		825 Hz	8+2+5=15=6 +	
	963 Hz	9+6+3=18=9 -		936 Hz	9+3+6=18=9 -	
4th Beast	1173 Hz	1+1+7+3=12=3		1146 Hz	1+1+4+6=12=3	4th Beast
	1284 Hz	1+2+8+4=15=6 +		1257 Hz	1+2+5+7=15=6 +	
	1395 Hz	1+3+9+5=18=9 -		1368 Hz	1+3+6+8=18=9 -	

Four beast (beats/beast anagram) contain 6 wings or tones in the 24 elders.

Rev. 4:8 And the **four beasts** had each of them **six wings** about him; and they were full of eyes within: and they rest not day and night, saying, Holy, holy, holy, Lord God Almighty, which was, and is, and is to come.

METATRON'S CUBE

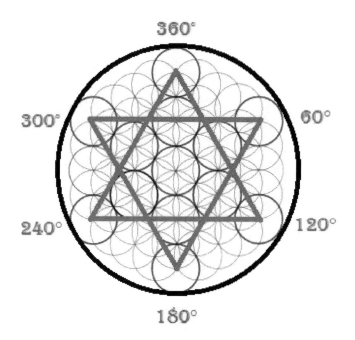

THE STAR OF DAVID
IN THE
CIRCLE OF DEGREES

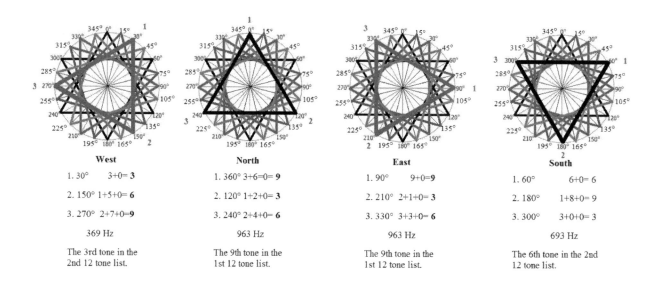

West

1. 30°   3+0= **3**

2. 150° 1+5+0= **6**

3. 270° 2+7+0=**9**

369 Hz

The 3rd tone in the
2nd 12 tone list.

North

1. 360° 3+6=0= **9**

2. 120° 1+2+0= **3**

3. 240° 2+4+0= **6**

963 Hz

The 9th tone in the
1st 12 tone list.

East

1. 90°   9+0=**9**

2. 210° 2+1+0= **3**

3. 330° 3+3+0= **6**

963 Hz

The 9th tone in the
1st 12 tone list.

South

1. 60°   6+0= 6

2. 180°   1+8+0= 9

3. 300°   3+0+0= 3

693 Hz

The 6th tone in the 2nd
12 tone list.

These are read in a clockwise direction.

144

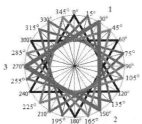

Book of Enoch CHAPTER XXXVI.

*Through each of these small portals pass the stars of heaven and run their course to the **west** on the **path which is shown to them.***

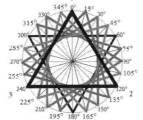

Book of Enoch CHAPTER XXXIV.

*1. And from thence I went towards the **north** to the ends of the earth, and there I saw a great and glorious device at the ends of the whole earth. 2. And here I saw **three portals** of heaven open in the heaven: through each of them proceed north winds: when they blow there is cold, hail, frost, snow, dew, and rain.*

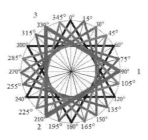

Book of Enoch CHAPTER XXXV.

*1. And from thence I went towards the west to the ends of the earth, and saw there **three portals** of the heaven open such as I had seen in the †east†, the same number of portals, and the same number of outlets.*

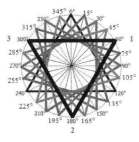

Book of Enoch CHAPTER XXXVI.

*1. And from thence I went to the **south** to the ends of the earth, and saw there **three open portals** of the heaven: and thence there come dew, rain, †and wind†.*

4 Star's of David or Solomon's Seal

Angles on a SOD is 60 degrees

Degree Circle with 15 Degree Intervals
24 Elders Around the Throne of God

	FIRST 12 TONES		**SECOND 12 TONES**	
1st Beast Lion	174 Hz	1+7+4=12=3	147 Hz	1+4+7=12=3
	285 Hz	2+8+5=15=6 +	258 Hz	2+5+8=15=6 +
	396 Hz	3+9+6=18=9 -	369 Hz	3+6+9=18=9 -
2nd Beast Calf	417 Hz	4+1+7=12=3	471 Hz	4+7+1=12=3
	528 Hz	5+2+8=15=6 +	582 Hz	5+8+2=15=6 +
	639 Hz	6+3+9=18=9 -	693 Hz	6+9+3=18=9 -
3rd Beast Man	741 Hz	7+4+1=12=3	714 Hz	7+1+4=12=3
	852 Hz	8+5+2=15=6 +	825 Hz	8+2+5=15=6 +
	963 Hz	9+6+3=18=9 -	936 Hz	9+3+6=18=9 -
4th Beast Eagle	1173 Hz	1+1+7+3=12=3	1146 Hz	1+1+4+6=12=3
	1284 Hz	1+2+8+4=15=6 +	1257 Hz	1+2+5+7=15=6 +
	1395 Hz	1+3+9+5=18=9 -	1368 Hz	1+3+6+8=18=9 -

Rev. 4:8 *And the **four beasts** had each of them **six wings** about him; and they were full of eyes within: and they rest not day and night, saying, **Holy, holy, holy,** Lord God Almighty, which was, and is, and is to come.* (4 beast/beats anagram, 6 wings/swings anagram (6 vertices of a Star of David) Holy-Gematria=60 degrees)

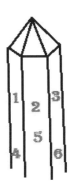

CRYSTALS HAVE 6 SIDES

Roberta Ruth Hill was born in Orlando, Florida. She graduated from High School in 1985 and has had two years of college. She became a CNA (Certified Nursing Assistant) in 1995. She has one son that is 23 years old. Roberta Hill is a home health care worker, writer and researcher. She has her own You Tube channel where she makes videos on the RH negative blood type, physics, astronomy, Coral Castle, poetry, animation, sacred geometry and various other subjects. Her channel is called TheStarchild2009. She has also written numerous online research books and poetry.

Made in the USA
Columbia, SC
25 June 2017